SpringerBriefs in Law

More information about this series at http://www.springer.com/series/10164

Marko Novak

The Type Theory of Law

An Essay in Psychoanalytic Jurisprudence

Springer

Marko Novak
European Faculty of Law
Nova Gorica, Slovenia

ISSN 2192-855X ISSN 2192-8568 (electronic)
SpringerBriefs in Law
ISBN 978-3-319-30642-1 ISBN 978-3-319-30643-8 (eBook)
DOI 10.1007/978-3-319-30643-8

Library of Congress Control Number: 2016938509

Printed on acid-free paper

This Springer imprint is published by Springer Nature
The registered company is Springer International Publishing AG Switzerland

Preface and Acknowledgments

I have always been fascinated with the duality of human nature. One such version is the duality that has existed in legal theory or legal philosophy from the very beginning of our civilization, that between natural law and legal positivism. Both perspectives have certainly proven to be persuasive accounts of law, but it needs to be understood how their authors can be so different as to have such distinct approaches concerning the essence of law. In order to obtain an insight into people's true nature, one needs to study psychology and I was very lucky to come into contact with Jung and his depth psychology. From amongst his enormous work in the field of analytical psychology, it was a particular typology that gave me at least a glimpse of understanding as to why people have such divergent views.

This book has been in a state of either gestation or writing for more than 10 years. In order to make a general account of something, one needs to develop an overarching perspective that can only be properly established over a longer period of time.

I have incorporated certain material from the following articles of mine, although with much revision and amplification: "A typological reading of prevailing legal theories", *Ratio Juris*, No. 2, Vol. 27 (2014) (Chaps. 1 and 3); "The argument from psychological typology for a mild separation between the context of discovery and the context of justification", in: Dahlman, C. (ed.), *Legal Argumentation Theory: Cross-Disciplinary Perspectives*, Dordrecht: Springer (2013) (Chap. 4); "Ideal Types of Law from the Perspective of Psychological Typology", *Revus*, No. 19 (2014) (Chap. 3); and "Legal Thinking: A Psychological Type Perspective", *Dignitas*, No. 49/50 (2011) (Chap. 2).

I would firstly like to thank Jože Magdič, who introduced me to Jung's work some 20 years ago and has since greatly encouraged my research and writing concerning Jung's psychological typology. I next need to acknowledge the support of Ivan Padjen, with whom I discussed some parts of my project and who helped in my research and development of the theory to some extent. My colleagues Luka Burazin, Giovanni Tuzet, Jernej Letnar Černič, Matej Avbelj, Vojko Strahovnik, and Hanna Maria Kreutzbauer were more than helpful with many a discussion we have had about my work, on the occasion of our several LegArg conferences at Nova Gorica, Bled, and Ljubljana. I also need to thank Rafael Manko, who was "on my side" at a conference in Zagreb. I would also like to acknowledge the support of John Mikhail from Georgetown University Law Center, who encouraged me to continue with my research of Jung. Moreover, I need to thank my English editors Dean DeVos, and particularly Aeddan Shaw, who has done the lion's share of the language editing.

Finally, this book would never have come to light were it not for the support of my beloved Romana, Luka Gal, and Vita.

Contents

Introduction

> Every judgment of an individual is limited by his or her type, and every manner of consideration is relative. Carl G. Jung (1962)

Individuals and their communities have always striven for some kind of balance, to harmonize conflicting tensions in themselves and also in their societies. Robert A. Johnson called this perennial search for balance "Balancing Heaven and Earth" (Johnson 1998), in order to emphasize that we balance, in ourselves and our societies, our everyday practical activities based on various rights and obligations against "higher" (metaphysical, moral, etc.) imperatives and aspirations, and vice versa. To address this never fully resolved problem, it seems that at some point people eventually began to make projections from the depths of their souls and thereby created the symbol of a goddess of justice holding in her arms scales, symbolizing the right balance between two opposing views. This craving for balance seems to be the same, regardless of time, place, and culture, and therefore universal. And, luckily, we do find it from time to time, if only for brief moments, to appease our introvertive and extravertive (social) battles of imbalance.

My ambition in this book is to shed light on a small aspect of this balance by focusing on legal ontology or questions such as where one should look for essence in law. I am aware of the fact that I am not going to find this essence since it constitutes a kind of Holy Grail, but I hope to at least point to where and how one might pursue it. In the history of legal philosophy, there seem to be two versions of the "Holy Grail": natural law and legal positivism. However, if the two had really been the "Holy Grail(s)" then the history of legal philosophy would have ended. Obviously this has not happened and so our search has to continue.

In accordance with Arthur Kaufmann, what is typical for the postmodern era is the ontological polarity between being and ought (Kaufmann 1993). Following him, in the framework of such an ontological model, being and ought are not strictly separated but are in a polar relation. This seems to be relieving news as it gives hope for (re)conciliation. In my opinion, this polar relationship might also seem to be a kind of integration or inclusiveness: an integration of quite conflicting views. If being and ought are able to be reconciled then also the opposing views of strict natural law, such as the ought which stems from the very nature of being, and of strict positive law being the ought adopted on the basis of people's interests, could be integrated to some extent.

In this essay in psychoanalytic jurisprudence, as I apply Jungian psychological typology to the above mentioned area of jurisprudence, I have tried to show how the integral or inclusive approach to understanding the nature of law is not only in tune with our (still postmodern?) time but also relevant for presenting a more persuasive picture of law than the older exclusivist or dualist approaches of strict natural law and rigid legal positivism. It is simply more persuasive as it is more realistic to take into consideration our whole psychological typology, how we act as a personality, and does not only point to our only one dimension as the one representing our true self. Once we truly understand this holistic perspective of multidimensionality, one-dimensionalism necessarily becomes reductionist.

In taking this multidimensional approach to law why then are Jung and his psychological type theory important for describing the nature of law? To try to answer this quite complex question I must, firstly, explain why psychoanalysis or psychology in general is important for legal theory or legal philosophy; secondly, why one should rely particularly on psychological typology as a special field of this very broad scientific discipline; and, thirdly, why one should opt for Jungian typology.

As to the first issue, after the modern discovery of psychology in the nineteen century, as a relatively young science in the overall history of (modern) sciences, although there had already been quite a few psychological attempts to describe a human being in the antiquity, it seems that there was no way back in trying to describe individual or social phenomena. Or, at least, the psychological approach in science has established itself to be a very important one. In legal theory or legal philosophy, we have had the very fruitful tradition of American Legal Realists, and particularly Jerome Frank (Frank 1930) as one of their important protagonists, who considered psychology or, more specifically, psychoanalysis as a very important area to give a glimpse of what goes on in respect of law and lawyers, judges, or other legal professionals when they deal with law. Moreover, their heirs, proponents of the Critical Legal Studies movement, used psychoanalysis, particularly Freudian, in order to criticize mainstream (liberal) law. Thus, when we try to describe law from a realist perspective, which is also my ambition here, it seems that psychology, or its upshot psychoanalysis, seems to be a logical choice to make.

Concerning the second tenet of the above-posed question, it seems that typology with its whole array of different categories that are very structured logically and linguistically in order to fully define a certain phenomenon. Let us remember Weber's famous typological interpretation of general legal history (Weber 1978) and how persuasive it was also from the position of the sociology of law, too. It was a superb description of law from the historical and sociological perspective, and this is also the reason why psychological typology was a choice to be made once I decided to rely on psychoanalysis. Law is a social discipline whereas psychology and psychoanalysis are humanist. Normally I take that into consideration as I analyze, firstly, the meaning of typology for the individual as *homo juridicus* (Supiot 2007). However, since law is needless for an individual and only makes sense in a society, secondly, I had to make a typological shift from individual to society when linking psychological typology with law and jurisprudence.

That collective (or social) understanding of psychological typology was not alien to Jung, whose psychological typology I have taken as my starting point in this research. Jung discussed his types very much substantively, almost archetypally – in short, philosophically. I am also taking as a similar approach here when I try to understand law and lawyers from the typological perspective. Jung understood such as metaphysical principles or ideas which really form the fundamental bases of everything we are and do. Through such types, I argue that we can much better understand ourselves, our role, and position in society.

After this introductory chapter, since this writing is mainly about jurisprudence, the book opens with Chap. 1 entitled "Integral Theories of Law." It is about those legal theories, nowadays quite frequent in this "postmodern" time, which search for the nature or essence of law beyond the classical positions of natural law and legal positivism. They came to the world arena of legal theory, particularly after World War II. Another name has recently begun to be used, namely inclusive theories of law, in order to distinguish them from the so-named exclusive theories of law which include strict natural law and strict legal positivism. From amongst these integral or inclusive legal theories I was most attracted by the three-dimensional theory of law, which I would like to explain here by virtue of its psychological typology and then extend in order for it to become a four-dimensional type theory of law. Moreover, since for the jurisprudential re-interpretation of this theory of law, I have resorted to Jungian psychological typology, as one of the greatest psychoanalysts of our time, this essay, to find it a legal theory context, should fall within works from the province of psychoanalytic jurisprudence.

Chapter 2 entitled "Understanding Law and Legal Practice through Jungian Type Theory," first, outlines the fundamentals of Jungian psychological types, initially how and to what extent they were developed by Jung, and, second, how they were continued by his followers, the position of which I try to assess critically returning, for the purpose of this book, to the original Jung and his position with respect to the types. Third, by analyzing the two attitudes (introversion and extraversion) as well as the four cognitive functions (thinking, feeling, sensation, and intuition) in the context of different legal professions I try to understand their specific role, particularities, advantages, and disadvantages in legal business. Fourth, I apply Jungian psychological typology (Jung 1921) to what I call (world) legal geography or comparative law, where I try to demonstrate how different (collective) psychological typologies have contributed to different legal systems and their peculiarities.

In Chap. 3, in a similar manner to the case of comparative law, I discuss the role of psychological typology in terms of legal history in the course of which different type models of law have been established depending on a particular psychological typology that was predominant at a certain time. These historical types express how the cognitive functions of individuals have contributed to law creation and law application in history. I conclude this chapter by criticizing these particular historical types of law from the position of a universal and general type theory of law that I develop at the end of this book.

Chapter 4 brings a discussion on how the different cognitive types influence the existence of different views on what is the question of the nature of law, or legal ontology. We will see that it is mainly due to the legal theorists' different predominant cognitive functions that we deal with different legal ontologies such as positive law and natural law, as well as with more contemporary ones that incorporate inclusive and exclusive positivist and non-positivist outlooks of the essence of law. The main focus is here, however, on the psychological-typological understanding of inclusive legal theories and then in particular the three-dimensional theory of law.

In Chap. 5, I add a fourth dimension to the classical three-dimensional theory of law, namely feeling, and discuss its role in today's law, particularly when it extends to the area of alternative dispute resolution. Furthermore, in the continuation of this chapter, I elaborate upon the major elements of what I call the type theory of law and then explain why I consider it to be a general and descriptive theory rather than a normative theory. I conclude this chapter by presenting the essential elements of a theoretical model of the type theory of law, and then demonstrating how it could be applied in the context of a controversial social, political, and legal issue which arose in an EU country in the area of constitutional law.

References

Frank, J. (1930). *Law and the modern mind.* Bretano's, Inc.

Johnson, R. A. (1998). *Balancing heaven and earth: A memoir of visions, dreams, and realizations.* HarperOne.

Jung, C. G., & Jaffé, A. (1965). *Memories, dreams, reflections.* New York: Random House (Original publication: 1962. *Erinnerungen, Träume, Gedanken.* Ekslibris).

Jung, C. G. (1971). *Psychological types.* London: Routledge (Original publication: 1921. *Psychologische Typen.* Duesseldorf: Patmost Verlag GmbH & Walter).

Kaufmann, A. (1993). *Einführung in Rechtsphilosophie und Rechtstheorie der Gegenwart.* Muller, Jur. Verlag.

Supiot, A. 2007. *Homo Juridicus, On the anthropological function of the law.* London/New York: Verso.

Weber, M. (1978). *Economy and society.* Berkeley: University of California Press.

Chapter 1
Integral Theories of Law

Abstract Integral theories of law, nowadays quite frequent in this "postmodern" time, search for the nature or essence of law beyond the classical positions of natural law and legal positivism, entering the world arena of legal theory largely after World War II. Another name has recently begun to be used, namely inclusive theories of law, in order to distinguish them from the so-called exclusive theories of law which include strict natural law and strict legal positivism. These theories seem to offer a more accurate account of law than exclusivist theories, the latter being reductionist in comparison with the former. From amongst these integral or inclusive legal theories, the three-dimensional theory of law is very interesting to me and which I explain by virtue of psychological typology. Since for the jurisprudential re-interpretation of this theory of law I have resorted to Jungian psychological typology, to find it a legal theory context this essay should fall within the realm of works from the province of psychoanalytic jurisprudence.

Keywords Integral theories of law • Inclusive theories of law • Three-dimensional theory of law • Jung • Psychological typology • Psychoanalytic jurisprudence

1.1 In General

Integral or synthetic, today most often called inclusivist, theories of law became relevant for a more comprehensive understanding of law particularly after World War II. This is hardly surprising since, after the horrors of the war, law was seen in a new light, including the views of post-war legal theorists and legal philosophers. In this context at least two prominent legal philosophers and their accounts of law are to be mentioned, the first from the legal family of civil law and the second from the legal tradition of common law. Having experienced the terror of Nazi law, e.g. in the form of the Nuremberg racial legislation, Gustav Radbruch departed from his previous rather more legal positivist approach to law (Radbruch 2003). His position towards the essence of law, which was argued in his later work, sought something of a synthesis or integration beyond legal positivism and natural law (Radbruch 1946). After this turning point, Radbruch influenced a significant number of largely continental legal theorists who sought a solution to the perennial conflict between natural law and legal positivism (see, e.g., Alexy 2002).

M. Novak, *The Type Theory of Law*, SpringerBriefs in Law,
DOI 10.1007/978-3-319-30643-8_1

Furthermore, Herbert Hart departed from his strict legal positivist predecessor, John Austin, to include at least a minimum content of morality into his positivist vision of law in his seminal work that was otherwise composed of legal rules (Hart 1961). In such a manner he became a role model for several generations of legal theorists, mostly from the common law legal tradition at first, who have sought the nature of law by transcending one-dimensional or exclusive approaches to law and thereby creating a kind of integration between positivist and moralist oriented fundamental features of law. These legal theorists increasingly began to be called 'inclusive legal positivists'.

Today what all sorts of legal synthetists, integralists, and inclusivists have in common, whilst not neglecting their perhaps important differences, is the distance that they wish to make from exclusivists or their one-sided approaches to understanding the essence of law. By their consideration of law's multiple dimensions as inherent to a proper account of law they surely regard exclusivist concepts of law as reductionist. To that extent I consider in this work integral, synthetic, and inclusive theories of law as synonymous attempts – in a very broad sense – to overcome the all too frequent expressions of the one-dimensionalism that is allegedly the most central to law. Conceptually, integration is quite close to inclusiveness when the idea of certain elements being integrated or included in a whole allows for the notion that, in such a whole, some elements may predominate over other elements. If that is the case then to use either integration or inclusiveness seems to be just playing with words. For that reason, since I see these two terms in that way, I most often use 'integration' as an overarching concept to also include inclusivist approaches to law.

Thus, what is the etymology of the adjective 'integral' and the noun 'integration'? The Latin word *integratio* implies gathering, combining, linking into a (n integral) whole. When we deal with integration or integrating we necessarily imply that there are several (at least two) dimensions or elements that integrate. Moreover, such integral whole cannot be understood without every individual element or dimension integrated into it while at the same time, being part of integration, no individual element can be comprehended alone without their whole. This implies a somewhat pluralist but more importantly also holistic perspective that could be referred to the concept of law too. Thus an integral theory of law would be a theory which would aim at describing the essence (or nature) of law by referring to its several dimensions which are necessarily integrated into a whole. Law as a whole cannot be properly understood without all of these elements being properly reflected upon. Only such a whole together can constitute a specific theory of law. Such an integral theory of law could include two, three, four, or even more dimensions. As already mentioned, what is important is that such a theory is an attempt at surpassing the deficiencies of the so-called reductionist theories of law (i.e. rigid or exclusive versions of non-positivism (or natural law) and legal positivism).

What I am trying to develop here is a specific theory of law, which is a special version of integral theory. But why this account of law cannot also be considered as a concept of law? Both theory and concept are able to describe a broader understanding of law. Theory (Greek *theoria*) entails abstract rumination and (usually introspective) reflection based on observing data. It is a process of arriving at certain conclusions about something. In my opinion theory seems to have a broader meaning in terms of developing (abstract) categories, and the connections thereof, than concept (Latin *conceptus* from *concipire*: to devise, form).[1] According to this perception, it is theory that can be composed of several concepts, and of their interrelations. Thus, for such a description of law as it is presented here, based on integration of several elements composing a whole, I have decided to use the term theory rather than concept.[2] Furthermore, in general theory of law we usually teach our students about fundamental legal concepts such as contract, statute, constitution, finality, legal remedy, etc. But there can also be a broader concept of law, which usually refers to its comprehensive definition or interpretation that unites all these narrow concepts. If we can have narrow and broad concepts in law it seems that the term theory is more comprehensive and overarching than concept in order to reflect on such a broad social phenomenon as law.

A next question is what should a theory encompass in order to be true or reliable account of what it is to present? Here we have some examples of its meaning from various legal theorists. According to Moreira Lima, "a theory must provide a scheme of systematic unification for previously disperse contents; it must offer a conceptual and symbolical representation of observed data; and it must offer a set of rules of inference which shall help in predicting the consequences of factual data" (Moreira Lima 110–111). Dickson furthermore suggests: "In short, analytical jurisprudence is concerned with explaining the nature of law by attempting to isolate and explain those features which make law into what it is." (Dickson 144). Moreover, a "successful theory of law of this type is a theory which consists of propositions about the law which (1) are necessarily true, and (2) adequately explain the nature of law" (Alexy 2004: 156–167). Finally, according to Van Hoecke "a theory in law is a system of coherent, non-contradictory assertions, views and concepts concerning some legal system or part of it, which are worded in such a way that it is possible to deduct from them testable hypotheses about the existence (validity) and interpretation of legal concepts, rules or principles" (Van Hoecke 15).

Accordingly, it seems that these legal theorists want to say that a theory must imply a coherent and consistent account of a certain phenomenon, which in its comprehensiveness is more the matter of weight and persuasion than of some formal limits and boundaries.

Before I proceed with developing my own integral theory of law as the type theory of law I will briefly discuss below how the legal inclusivists disagree with legal exclusivists on certain important aspects of law. After all, inclusiveness is quite a popular term in contemporary jurisprudence so it seems appropriate to discuss it in a few lines and to try to see how it departs from exclusiveness in

[1] Further, conceptions I consider as being constitutive of a particular concept.

[2] *Cf.* the concept of law developed by Hart in his The Concept of Law.

jurisprudence. It is also very close to what I understand under integration in terms of linking the fundamentals of psychological typology with jurisprudence.[3]

In the next few paragraphs I will first link the exclusivist and then the inclusivist views of law with some of the basics of psychology or even psychological typology as developed by Carl G. Jung (Jung 1971). Some more detailed elements of Jung's typology will be presented below.

1.2 Exclusive and Inclusive Legal Theories

Historically, rationality in law has had two predominant meanings that were reflected in the corresponding legal theories. In their extreme or exclusivity, we consider natural law theories as falling within exclusive rationalism, and legal positivism as within exclusive or extreme empiricism.

First, those who supported a metaphysical-rational epistemological approach to law, either in its older version (such as Lao-Tzu, Confucius, Aristotle, Cicero, and Aquinas) or in its modern version (e.g. Geny, Dabin, Cohen, Fuller, and Finnis) (Prakash Sinha 1993, V–XII), found the true law in rational principles that are accessible to persons through their ability to grasp and understand certain internal idea(l)s, such as God, nature, morality, etc. As already mentioned, such a manner of operation of the human mind that is directed at the overall connectedness of knowledge and the possibility of ideas has traditionally been considered as 'intellect' (lat. *intellectus*). Below we will see that such rationality was mostly influenced by intuition, as a cognitive function, and might thus be called intuitive rationality.

The second understanding of the 'rational' refers to *ratio* or to the capacity of abstracting, differentiating, analyzing, making concepts, of applying means to ends (the so-called instrumental (Horkheimer 1974) or empirical rationality). Such approaches to legal theory have traditionally been labelled as empiricist-positivistic epistemological approaches to an understanding of the concept of law (especially positivistic theories of law) (Prakash Sinha 1993). Such views mostly appeared at the beginning of modernity and have to some degree been extended to the present.

Jung, on whom I rely very much in this book with respect to his psychological typology, accepted William James's differentiation between the "rationalist" and the "empiricist" as between intellectualism and empiricism. The rationalist is more idealistic and dogmatic, while the empiricist is more skeptical and materialist. The rationalist begins with the whole and what is universal and unites things within a perspective, whereas the empiricist begins with parts and makes a set of parts out of the whole within a pluralistic perspective. In his opinion the difference between

[3] The reader will notice that, in the most parts of this book, I use different concepts such as legal theory, legal philosophy, and jurisprudence interchangeably for the purpose of rather broadly theoretically reflect on the phenomenon of law, finding no particular reason to make the said distinctions.

intuitive thinking, as the thinking which obtains data most importantly from intuition, and empirical thinking, as the thinking that acquires data from the senses, is the basis for another dichotomy that is typical of the natural law tradition and the positivistic law tradition, i.e. methodological monism and methodological pluralism (Jung 1971: 221).

Thus, according to Jung, monism is a position that is oriented toward an idea. An idea is always of a hierarchical character whether it is obtained on the basis of abstraction from a representation and concrete occurrences, or exists *a priori* as an unconscious form. In the first example it is the highest point of everything that is embraced and determined by such, while in the second example it is the unconscious "legislature" that regulates the possibilities and necessities of thinking. In every case it is dominant. Even if there are several ideas, one of them predominates for a certain period of time (Jung 1971: 233–34). Such ideas in the natural law traditions have been, for example, God, nature, spirit, morality, (high) Reason, etc. For example, in Aquinas the first principles of natural law were indemonstrable (Aquinas I–II, 94, a. 5, c, ad. 3; Clark 2000). In Plato the idea of the Good was above everything, in Aristotle such idea is Nature. Accordingly, people may have insights into intuitive-intellectual principles that are inborn in our minds (such as moral consciousness). Furthermore, following such a perspective, there is a certain internal or inborn necessity that people must follow when carrying out their acts and regulating their relations with other people. Such knowledge is accessible for evaluation through intuition, which has access to our internal "truths". In terms of modern natural law theories, this internal necessity would be morality or moral principles. According to such an exclusivist version, everything must be subjected to a principle.

On the contrary, a pluralist conception is based on the sense experience of the outer world that is not "pre-regulated" by a certain internal necessity, but is completely free from it. So there is nothing predetermined inside us, rather we are "clean slates" and the knowledge that we acquire depends solely on the experiences gained through our senses. What we acquire from own senses are positivistic experiences. Accordingly, the position that is externally oriented toward the object always has a tendency to a multiplicity of concepts and principles, without which only one explanation cannot be adjusted to the essence of the object (Jung 1971: 234).

Nevertheless, today, among the exclusive or 'pure' legal theories there exists so-called exclusive legal positivism, which entails a necessary exclusion of morality from the ambit of the concept of law (Raz 1979: 47). This maintains that due to certain moral defects, the legal validity of the laws containing such moral defects is never lost (Alexy 2008: 287). What is sharply contrasted with such is so-called exclusive legal non-positivism, which entails the necessary inclusion of morality in the concept of law or its non-necessary exclusion from such a concept. In accordance with such a viewpoint, due to certain moral defects, the legal validity of the laws containing such moral defects is always lost (Alexy, *ibid.*).

Let me repeat that in particular after World War II the exclusivist natural law and legal positivistic theoretical approaches were gradually replaced by those which tended to overcome the one-sidedness of strict natural law and legal positivism. In this context I have already mentioned the works of Radbruch and Hart, to name just two of the greatest legal philosophers. On the basis of such attempts at finding a third way beyond exclusive natural law and legal positivism towards certain inclusivist perspectives, the division between exclusivist and inclusivist legal theories was born.

The mentioned legal theorists started from the fact that law as a human experience cannot be reduced only to so-called exclusive perceptions of the legal world. On one hand, there is the exclusive perception of natural law theories, which to a great extent subordinate the perception of people to intuitive thinking as the kind of thinking that mainly, or to a very important extent, acquires data or information from intuition. In terms of law, this entails that what is perceived through such intuition are, for example, internal laws of nature or moral principles that have precedence over the rules set by the positive legislature. On the other hand there is the exclusive perception of theories of legal positivism that subordinate human perception to empirical thinking, as the kind of thinking which obtains the most relevant information from the senses. As already indicated, in contradistinction to intuitive (or moral) laws that are mostly internally perceived, positive laws are perceived empirically. In case of a conflict between the two, natural lawyers would give priority to the former, while legal positivists would to the latter.

I have also indicated that those legal theorists who want to overcome the exclusivity of the mentioned two epistemological perspectives can be named syntheticists or integralists. In order to overcome the exclusivity of the classical (or "pure") legal theories as described above, they tend to accept the idea of inclusivity. Such inclusivity is close to what otherwise is perceived as synthetic or integral. Such integration tries to find an exit from the dilemma whether to accept the exclusivity of a traditional natural law perspective or legal positivist perspective. Ontologically, the idea of inclusivity is founded on methodological polarity as the connecting and intertwining of being (*Sein*) and the ought (*Sollen*), i.e. the factual and the normative. It seeks an exit from the dilemma of methodological monism and methodological dualism. According to Kaufmann, methodological polarity is a typical postmodern perspective (Kaufmann 1993: 130). As already stated, we find legal inclusivity both in legal positivist and legal non-positivist circles.

My theory of law as an integral theory certainly stems from the tradition of inclusivist theories of law. According to psychological typology, the individual is not a one-dimensional subject but necessarily a totality of various aspects and dimensions, as is society as well as law as its important phenomenon. This also follows from the three-dimensional theory of law as presented below, with which I find quite a few (but not all) overlapping points.

1.3 A Three-Dimensional Theory of Law

One of the world's most famous integral theories of law was surely the three-dimensional theory of law as developed by the Brazilian thinker Miguel Reale. There have been other (older) authors who also dealt with some kind of three-dimensional theory of law, such as Kantorowicz, Pound, Duguit. For a more modern approach, see Hall (1964, 1976). Moreover, a recent very interesting account of three-dimensionality in law can be found in Falcón y Tella (2010: 13), where she dissects the three-dimensionality in law into the following categories: (a) structural three-dimensionalism (facts, norms, values); (b) three-dimensionalism of principles (causality, attribution, liberty); (c) anthropological three-dimensionalism (individual, citizen, person); (d) epistemological three-dimensionalism ((i) legal knowledge: philosophy of law – deontology, legal dogmatics – logic; sociology of law – phenomenology; (ii) legal philosophical knowledge: theory of justice (working), theory of law (being), theory of legal science (knowing); (iii) perspectives in legal theory: theory of the legal norm, theory of the legal order, theory of the legal relationship).

Reale's three-dimensional theory of law[4] contends that law is a very comprehensive phenomenon that cannot be reduced to only one dimension but necessarily reflects the co-existence of three dimensions: legal values, legal facts, and legal norms. These three dimensions of law are subject of three distinct disciplines: natural law, sociology of law, and legal positivism (Reale 2003: 121). For Reale only the combination of these three dimensions provides a complete account of law. This is achieved through the concept of dialectics of complementarity (Reale 1977). Law is always value, fact and norm and the relation between them is formed dialectically. "Although it is true that one of the three dimensions may at one point be prevalent ... one dimension will always be a function of the other two dimensions." (Moreira Lima 137–38).

Reale's dialectics originate from Husserl's understanding of *Lebenswelt* (life-world). This signifies incessant dynamism in which opposing concepts continue to co-exist and a solution is not necessarily reached (Moreira Lima 121). Reale's dialectics of complementarity being his understanding of Husserl's lifeworld is a world in which terms do "not evolve to superior categorized forms but is a constant existential condition, the content of which varies incessantly, but never ceases to exist as the great social container, in which we can find the individuals with their works and institutions" (Reale 1977: XXVII).

Husserl's *Lebenswelt* is filled with dynamism and avoids an objective, absolute truth. For Reale law is but one of the dimensions of human life, and legal models are always subject to changes within the *Lebenswelt*. For him dialectics does not focus

[4] His most important book in which he developed this theory is entitled *Teoria tridimensional do direito* [Three-dimensional Theory of Law] from 1968. Since very few works of Reale were published in English, for a concise but very instructive work in English on his three-dimensional theory of law see Moreira Lima (2008).

on identifying polar and contradictory terms. So the evolution described in his three-dimensional theory of law is similar or parallel to the changes in the *Lebenswelt* (Moreira Lima 122–124).

Furthermore, according to Reale: "In the realm of the dialectics of complementarity opposites are implicated into each other to the extent necessary to reveal that the contradiction was only apparent, but such revelation will not prevent the opposites from continuing to be contraries, each of such opposites are identical to themselves and involved in mutual and necessary correlation" (Reale 1977: 120). Moreover, "within the dialectics of complementarity, there is a permanent and ever progressing relationship between two or more factors, which cannot be understood separately from each other" (Reale 1977: 188). Terms that are contrary to each other can be reconciled (through dialectical processes) but not terms that contradict each other (Moreira Lima 128).

Where does Jung and his psychological typology fit into such integral theories of law?

Once I describe Jung's type theory, in the introductory part of the following chapter, I will connect integral theories of law, particularly the three-dimensional theory of law, with Jung's psychological typology. Thus we will see how understanding Jung's type theory is important for a proper consideration not only of that theory but legal theories in general. Psychological type theory demonstrates that our comprehension of the world and its phenomena must be multi-dimensional if we want to approach as epistemologically true a nature of the world as possible, and also a more true nature of law. In that light we will be able to see why exclusivist theories of law, that more or less base their picture of law on only one dimension, have so many shortcomings. They simply deny a more proper nature of a human being with all of his or her multi-dimensions.

However, as already indicated, my type theory of law not only follows but also departs to some extent from Reale's multi-dimensional account of law, which follows in the continuation of this book, in Sect. 4.3.

Before I begin discussing the fundamentals of Jung's type theory and translate it into a legal theory through an integral approach to law, let us stop for a moment at explaining a few basic tenets about a great tradition of intersections between psychoanalysis and law, in the framework of which the type theory of law as developed here necessarily belongs.

1.4 Psychoanalytic Jurisprudence

1.4.1 Law and Psychology

As with every other human activity, law seems to be nothing but a reflection of the operation of the human mind in a certain manner. Such reflection demonstrates how a person's (subject's) state of mind is projected on a certain object or a certain area of activity. Consequently, in order to learn what a certain object is, or how it appears, we must study the psychological characteristics of the persons who deal with such, i.e. who create and apply it. Law and legal norms are part of the social reality in which people create and apply legal norms. In this way they project and thus objectify their internal, and thus subjective, interests, motives, desires, moral standards as their necessarily psychic experiences.

Although certain psychological studies of the individual psyche had already been conducted in Ancient Greece (for example, by the most prominent philosophers such as Plato and Aristotle), more thorough scientific psychological research only began in modern times. It is related to the greater interest on the part of science in the internal or subjective aspects of people. From among the classical sciences, psychology has been established as one of the most recent. However, its establishment greatly influenced other sciences and art. Inside psychology in general, psychoanalysis also had an important impact on people's reflection of their scientific, professional and artistic activities. Here one needs to mention Sigmund Freud in particular and his findings about the human psyche, and certainly one should not neglect Carl Gustav Jung.

It seems that after the (modern) "discovery" of psychology, which as a rule bases its findings on self-reflection, we can no longer avoid relating our acts and activities to the structure of our mind. According to Jung, what our ancestors had noticed on the "sky" (which included the entire Old Greek Pantheon) was nothing other than the substance of their collective unconsciousness, i.e. the archetypes as forces which gave shape and sense to people's living on the earth (Pascal 1994: 84). When translating the aforementioned into a relation of psychology and law, following Leon Petrażycki, the founder of the psychological theory of law, law and morality really exists only in an individual psyche, in which the norms, i.e. rights and duties, are only projections that originate from their inclination to objectify the substance of their psychological experiences (Motyka 2007).

The increased importance of psychology and psychoanalysis on other scientific disciplines led to its influence on the study of law. In such a manner, the special scientific fields of forensic psychology and psychopathology were developed in the framework of which individual psychological elements in court proceedings and judicial trials are the subject of interest. From this foundation, the disciplines of psychology of the defendant, the witness, etc., were developed. Here, however, I am not so much interested in conducting psychological experimental analysis but rather on applying certain psychoanalytical findings to a philosophical understanding of law. Thus the concept of 'psychoanalytic jurisprudence' is very much in place in terms of what I am interested in doing here. Thus, my methodological approach is one which is typical of legal philosophy or legal ontology since the essence or nature of law tries to be found through the psychological characteristic of lawyers and other people dealing with law, these being the figures who mostly define the contents and scope of law. To an important extent this occurs through the projection of their psychological characteristics to the processes of law making and the application of law. We could maintain that law as a social creation does not stem from a world that is external to the society but necessarily originates from it. In this manner it reflects the psychological characteristics of those people who have created and applied it.

Psychological studies are not new for legal philosophy. Psychological and psychoanalytic considerations were very much included in the work of representatives of the school of legal realism, both in the United States and Scandinavia. Among those particularly interested in psychology concerning law were Jerome Frank and Axel Hagerström (Mindus 2009) and in this context I have already mentioned Petrażycki (Petrazycki 2011).

1.4.2 Psychoanalysis, Law, and Jung

Frank was one of the protagonists of the intellectual movement of the American Legal Realists (hereinafter ALR). Frank, who at some point in his career was a judge, looked at the concept of law from a psychoanalytical perspective. In his work Frank addressed certain psychological specialties of an individual that might affect the (excessive) emotionality of his or her judgments (e.g. impatience, irrational irritation when faced with unpleasant thoughts that refer to wishes, hatred, the sense of power, loyalty to certain groups) (Frank 1930: 206).

According to Frank, law is uncertain, indefinite and subject to unpredictable changes. However, such uncertainty about law is not an unfortunate fact but an important social value since otherwise society would be too tightly restricted and unable to adjust to the reality of incessant social, economic and political changes (Frank 1930: 207–08).

Furthermore, Frank asserted that in terms of psychology the process of adjudication rarely begins at the upper syllogistic premise, on the basis of which the judge only deduces or makes an inference. Quite the contrary, Frank opined that judges generally make their judgments in the opposite direction, i.e. stemming from speculative conclusions made in advance. Judgments are thus based on judges' internal premonitions. He called such premonitions or stimuli hunch producers, which as political, economic and moral prejudices tell the judges to reach certain decisions that are formally based on rules and principles. According to Frank, there are also other hunches and premonitions that depend on the characteristics of an individual judge who is to make certain conclusions or decisions. Therefore, in Frank's opinion, a judge's personal traits, his or her psychological dispositions, prejudices, sympathies and antipathies (in relation to, e.g., witnesses or parties to proceedings) decide on what is to be the right decision in a particular case. From this perspective, the judge does not differ from other "mortals" (Frank 1930: 207–08).

According to Frank, following such use of intuition, the judge *a posteriori* begins to apply rational arguments in order to check (or supervise) whether it is possible by such to justify the conclusion that was *a priori* made by virtue of his or her intuition. This entails that the conclusion made in advance, or *a priori*, essentially determines the arguments used in the reasoning. In Frank's opinion, if this is not possible, then the judge will have to choose another conclusion except he or she is "arbitrary or insane" (Frank 1930: 203).

Following Frank if we wish to know something more about hunches that contribute to lawmaking we should know the judge's personality. Thus, law changes in accordance with the personality of a judge that decides on a certain case. However, such a distinction between judges cannot be disclosed in connection with the writing of their judgments particularly due to their ability to use different tricks in order to disguise disharmony between them. In such a manner, true irrational inclinations are hidden behind the veil of a rational structure of reasoning. However, from time to time we learn something about judges' personal preferences only through their interviews, biographies, literary works about them, as well as from brilliant and bad reasoning of their decisions. Although rules and principles are foundations of law they are only instigations for the activity of judges. Accordingly, Frank was certain that the main factor in the operation of law is a judge's personality (Frank 1930: 206).

Frank's ideal was a fully grown-up lawyer (judge) who does not need external authority but possesses constructive doubt that enables him or her to create law in accordance with a developing civilization. At the same time, such a judge is (to be) aware of his or her prejudices, take(s) them into consideration, and deal(s) with such rationally in order to achieve a decision that would be as just (and objective) as possible (Frank 1930: 212).

Following Frank, judges necessarily have discretion when they apply abstract rules to concrete facts, i.e. they necessarily create law by making value judgments, since legal creativity is the essence of the life of law. According to Frank, the ideal judge would not abuse power but take care of the enforcement of justice by applying their knowledge of law and being aware of their potential prejudices and weaknesses (i.e. his or her human nature) (Frank 1930: 210).

In general the ALR have criticized legal formalists or legal positivists who claim that law or law application is (fully) determined by mere legal provisions, in the framework of which (according to the most extreme position, that of German mechanical jurisprudence) judges are to be completely neutral (even mechanical) "technicians" who merely apply abstract legal norms to concrete facts.[5] The main tasks of the ALR were certainly to destroy the myth pointing to such full (even scientific) autonomy of law and the narrowly perceived empiricist's perception of the application of law.

I am very much aware of the ALR's valuable contributions to disclosing the idea that law and a lawyer's psychological predisposition are interconnected, and that law is merely a result of the projection of lawyers' activities when creating or applying the law. I agree with their perspective that law can be indeterminate as it depends on, e.g., judges as human beings, and also on how the law is interpreted and applied in a particular case. This certainly proves the fact that a judge is necessarily

[5] The greatest extreme of such an "empirical" approach to law was the General Land Law for the Prussian States from 1794 containing no fewer than 17,000 paragraphs (Zweigert, Kötz 138).

subjective when adjudicating cases, but this subjectivity, such as judge's hunches (intuitive ideas), are not necessarily something bad if they are taken in the overall context of the profession of a judge as a responsible actor.

The ALRs were scientifically active in the period between the two world wars, and were particularly influenced by Freud's psychoanalytical theory. Furthermore, Freud was a source of inspiration for much of postmodern legal thought (e.g. French structuralism, deconstruction). He also had a considerable impact on the Critical Legal Studies (hereinafter the CLS) movement (Caudill 1991) who claimed the ALR to have been one of their sources of inspiration. However, it seems that the CLS proponents did not take from the ALR the position that irrationality in law can also be positive, not necessarily negative.

Here we need to add another great psychoanalyst, Jacques Lacan, who was importantly influenced by Freud, and his important influence on poststructuralism, critical social theory and critical legal theory (see, *e.g.*, Caudill 1997).

However, there was not much interest from the great legal theorists in another great psychoanalyst, Jung, and his analytical psychology. To some extent this is even understandable, since many of Jung's writings touched upon areas which are quite slippery (e.g. alchemy, parapsychology) for law and legal theory that more focus on clarity, determinacy, externality, formality and rationality. To some the psychoanalytical thought should be in complete contradiction to the legal thinking that tries to categorize and divide instead of making integration, and try to rationalize instead of taking into account also, e.g., emotions in legal decision-making. Thus, one author wrote: "Law is a system that is intended for transferring grey into black and white whereas psychoanalysis is, to the contrary, meant to reshape black and white into grey" (Duncan 1994: 725, 799).

Despite the above-mentioned factors there are parts of Jung's work which could be more directly important for an understanding of the work of lawyers and law as such. For this reason this book focuses on his theory of psychological types (Jung 1971), and its subsequent development and modification, as applying to the areas related to law, legal theory, and legal philosophy such as legal thinking or the particularities of thinking in various legal professions, legal argumentation, legal philosophy and legal ontology.

We saw above that with the emergence of psychoanalysis between the two World Wars, and its development in various directions after World War II, psychoanalysis as a new discipline gradually began to influence legal theory too. Thus in recent decades the special term 'psychoanalytic jurisprudence' was fabricated (see, e.g., Ehrenzweig 1971) to join the two disciplines by mainly dealing with psychoanalytic interpretation of law and specific legal institutions. Although such psychoanalytic jurisprudents have predominantly consisted of the followers of Freud and Lacan, it seems necessary to also include Jungians under this quite general umbrella of psychoanalytic jurisprudence. What Jung and his thought can bring to this "club" through the contributions of his followers by virtue of their applying his very comprehensive ideas, on the edge of science, to the present social reality are new aspects and perspectives that can additionally illuminate our time of postmodern scientific orientation. These can be normally applied in the context of law as well and this book is one such attempt.

References

Alexy, R. (2002). *The argument from injustice*. Oxford: Oxford University Press.

Alexy, R. (2004). The nature of legal philosophy. *Ratio Juris, 17*(2), 156–167.

Alexy, R. (2008). On the concept and the nature of law. *Ratio Juris, 21*(3), 281–299.

Caudill, D. S. (1991). Freud and critical legal studies: Contours of a radical socio-legal psychoanalysis. *Indiana Law Journal, 66*(3), 651–697.

Caudill, D. S. (1997). *Lacan and the subject of law: Toward a psychoanalytic critical legal theory*. Atlantic Highlands: Humanity Books.

Clark, M. T. (2000). *An Aquinas reader*. New York: Fordham University Press.

Dickson, J. (2001). *Evaluation and legal theory: Or how to succeed in Jurisprudence without moral evaluation (Legal theory today)*. Oxford/Portland, Oregon: Hart Publishing.

Duncan, M. G. (1994). In slime and darkness: The metaphor in criminal justice. *Tulane Law Review, 68*(725), 799.

Ehrenzweig, A. A. (1971). *Psychoanalytic jurisprudence*. Dobbs Ferry, NY: Oceana Publications.

Falcón y Tella, M. J. (2010). *A three-dimensional theory of law*. Leiden: Martinus Nijhoff Publishers.

Frank, J. (1930). *Law and the modern mind*. New York: Bretano's Inc.

Hall, J. (1964). From legal theory to integrative jurisprudence. *University of Cincinnati Law Review, 33*, 153.

Hall, J. (1976). Integrative jurisprudence. *The Hastings Law Journal, 27*, 779.

Hart, H. L. A. (1961). *The concept of law*. Oxford: Oxford University Press.

Horkheimer, M. (1974). *Eclipse of reason*. London/New York: Continuum International Publishing Company Ltd.

Jung, C. G. (1971). *Psychological types*. London: Routledge.

Kaufmann, A. (1993). *Einführung in Rechtsphilosophie und Rechtstheorie der Gegenwart*. Heidelberg: Muller Jur. Verlag.

Mindus, P. (2009). *A real mind: The life and work of Axel Hagerstram*. Dordrecht: Springer.

Moreira Lima, A. C. (2008). A Brazilian perspective on Jurisprudence: Miguel Reale's tridimensional theory of law. *Oregon Review of International Law, 10*, 77–138.

Motyka, Karel. (2007). *Leon Petrazycki challenge to legal orthodoxy*. Cracow: 23rd IVR World Congress.

Pascal, E. (1994). *Jung to live by*. London: Souvenir Press.

Petrazycki, L. (2011). *Law and morality*. New Brunswick: Transaction Publishers.

Prakash Sinha, S. (1993). *Jurisprudence, legal philosophy*. St. Paul: West Publishing Co.

Radbruch, G. (1946). Gesetzliches Unrecht und übergezetzliches Recht. *Süddeutsche Juristenzeitung:* 105 *et seq.*

Radbruch, G. (2003). *Rechtsphilosophie*. Heidelberg: C. F. Müller.

Raz, J. (1979). *The authority of law: Essays on law and morality*. Oxford: Oxford University Press.

Reale, M. (1977). *Experiencia e cultura*. Sao Paolo: EDUSP.

Reale, M. (2003). *Teoria tridimensional do direito*. Sao Paulo: Editora Saraiva.

Van Hoecke, M. (Ed.). (2011). *Methodologies of legal research: Which kind of method for what kind of discipline?* Oxford/Portland, Oregon: Hart Publishing.

Zweigert, K., & Kötz, H. (1998). *Introduction to comparative law*. Oxford: Clarendon.

Chapter 2
Understanding Law and Legal Practice Through Jungian Type Theory

Abstract In this chapter I outline the fundamentals of Jungian psychological types, initially how and to what extent they were developed by Jung, and, second, how they were continued by his followers. The position of his followers concerning psychological typology, especially of those called "empirical post-Jungians," I try to assess critically by returning to Jung and his position with respect to the types. Furthermore, by analyzing the two attitudes (introversion and extraversion) as well as the four cognitive functions (thinking, feeling, sensation, and intuition) in the context of different legal professions I try to understand their specific role, particularities, advantages and disadvantages in legal business. Finally, I apply Jungian psychological typology to what I call (world) legal geography or comparative law, where I try to demonstrate how different (collective) psychological typologies have contributed to different legal systems and their peculiarities.

Keywords Fundamentals of Jungian psychological types • Post-Jungians • Attitudes • Cognitive functions • Legal professions • Comparative law

2.1 General Features of the Psychological Type Theory

2.1.1 Original Jung

Although categorizing people according to certain psychological types has an ancient origin, the most famous modern approach to psychological typology comes from Jung. There were, however, certain attempts from contemporary Jungian psychoanalysts (hereinafter the Post-Jungians) to extend his thought on psychological typology in a certain more empirical direction but they seem not to have been as successful as they had intended.

There were many influences from ancient and modern authors on Jung, and concerning psychological types there was a particular influence from William James (Jung 1971: 220–236).

James was one of those who opined that when a philosopher thinks, he or she necessary thinks a fact of his or her temperament. Thus he or she interprets the world according to his or her temperament since the structure of our psyche necessarily determines the way in which we see things. Following James, in

M. Novak, *The Type Theory of Law*, SpringerBriefs in Law,
DOI 10.1007/978-3-319-30643-8_2

philosophy there have always been two types of philosophers: the rationalist and the empiricist. Namely, a great historical division has existed between the empiricists (e.g. British philosophers such as Locke, Berkeley, and Hume) and the rationalists (e.g. continental thinkers such as Descartes, Leibniz, and Spinoza). The former held that all our knowledge must ultimately be derived, as is the case with the (natural) sciences, from our sense-experience, while the latter insisted that knowledge properly so called requires a direct insight or a demonstration, for which our faculty of reason in indispensable (Mautner 174–176).

According to James, the rationalist is in favor of abstract and internal principles, while what are most important for the empiricist are facts in all their variety. Although in every person both aspects are present, one or the other element predominates. For James, rationalism is synonymous with intellectualism, and empiricism with sensuality. The rationalist is more idealistic and dogmatic, while the empiricist is more skeptical and materialist. The rationalist begins with the whole and what is universal and unites things, while the empiricist begins with parts and makes a set of parts out of the whole. According to James, the rationalist is tender-minded (having a gentle and subtle spirit), whereas the empiricist is tough-minded (having a tough spirit). In addition, James saw the tender-minded as rational (the one who follows principles), intellectual, idealistic, optimistic, religious, indeterminate, monistic, and dogmatic. In contradistinction, he saw the tough-minded as empirical (following facts), sensual, materialistic, pessimistic, irreligious, deterministic, pluralistic, and skeptical. Finally, what is typical of the tough-minded is, following James, concrete thinking (based on the senses), while abstract thinking (based on ideas) is typical of the tender-minded (James 6–9).

Thus, Jung found many similarities with James's epistemology and even applied such in the development of his theory of types, which he developed much more than others so his is certainly to be considered one of the greatest theories of psychological types that was ever elaborated.

Jung's scientific opus is otherwise extremely vast and stretches to areas that are mostly less irrelevant to law that otherwise emphasizes clarity, determinateness, externality, formality, systematic character, and rationality. However, the field of psychological types seems to be an area of Jung's intellectual heritage that may also be interesting for law and lawyers. It deals with healthy, well-balanced personalities, not psychopathology. Thus, Jung's theory of psychological types provided me with a starting point for beginning to understand the role of psychological types in relation to the phenomena of law, lawyers and legal thinking.

Accordingly, here I am interested in establishing how different psychological types originally established by Jung have determined the character of law, lawyers and legal thinking. However, before I begin indicating possible connections between the basic psychological types and the main dimensions of law and legal thinking, I should outline some introductory elements of Jung's typological theory.

Initially, I should emphasize perhaps Jung's best known concepts of extraversion and introversion. These two basic "attitudes" describe how psychic energy is divided in human beings, where we prefer to focus our attention, and what energizes us. The extraverted attitude is motivated from the outside and is directed by external, objective factors and relationships. In the case of an extravert who gets energy from external elements, psychic energy flows outwards towards the world. Whereas in the case of an introvert, who mainly gets his or her energy from within and also withdraws energy from the world, e.g. from the world of ideas, inner, subjective facts, thoughts, interests, and imagination. Those who prefer extraverting get their energy from the outer world of people, external objects, excitements, activities, and things. Extraverts usually seek interaction, enjoy groups, act or speak first and then think, expend energy, focus outwardly, are talkative, like variety and action, are outgoing, think out loud, and enjoy discussing (Baron 10, 13).

However important these findings of Jung's on introversion and extraversion may have been for understanding the very nature of people's attitude, they are of marginal interest for me here because, to better understand law and legal practice, I think it is much more productive to focus on people's cognitive functions. In my opinion, these functions better define the substance of how people perceive and evaluate facts and legal norms in the framework of legal practice, and how they reflect on them when they elaborate legal theories. Still, when one deals with psychological typology it is impossible to completely neglect the attitudes.

In addition to the two attitudes already mentioned, Jung introduced four functional types or four (cognitive) functions of the psyche to describe the character of the psyche. Jung posited four functions of the psyche and grouped them into two pairs of opposites. On one hand, there are two rational or evaluative functions as they evaluate experience by helping us to make decisions: i.e. thinking and feeling. On the other hand, there are two irrational or perceptive functions: sensation and intuition, as they do not evaluate but depend on acts of perception by referring to how we prefer to take in information. By means of the irrational functions, we perceive objects, people, events, and ideas, while with the rational functions we evaluate what we have perceived with the irrational functions (Jung 1971) (Fig. 2.1).

Sensation tells us that something exists. Those who prefer sensing pay attention to information taken in directly through their five senses and focus on what is or what was. Sensors usually prefer facts, concrete information, are more interested in what is actual, pay attention to specifics, are practical and realistic, focus on the present, value common sense, and are pragmatic. Sensing notices the sights,

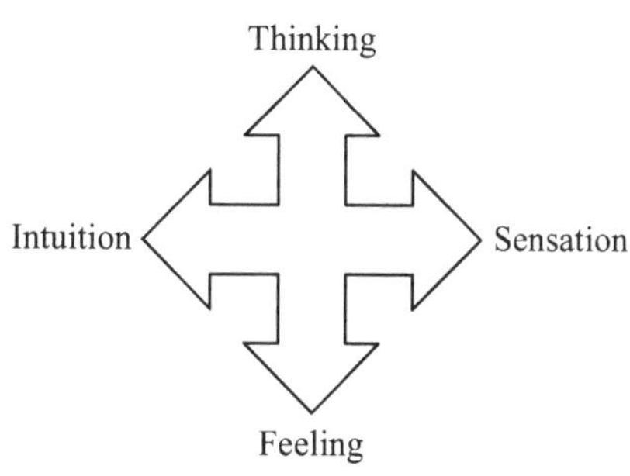

Fig. 2.1 Four (cognitive) functions of the psyche according to Jung

sounds, smells and all the sensory details of the present. It categorizes, organizes, records and stores the specifics from the here and now. It is reality-based, dealing with "what is". It also provides the specific details of memory and recollections from past events (Reinhold 2010).

Thinking tells us what it is. Those who prefer thinking make decisions in a logical and objective way. Our thinking analyses information in a detached, objective fashion. It operates from factual principles, deduces and forms conclusions systematically. Thinkers are usually firm minded, analyze the problem, are objective, convinced by logic, are direct, value competence, decide with their head, value justice, can be seen as insensitive, are good at critiquing, and usually do not take things personally (Jung 1971).

Further, feeling suggests that it is good or not. Those who prefer feeling make decisions in a personal, values-oriented way. They usually are gentle-hearted, sympathize with your problem, are subjective, convinced by values, are tactful, value relationships, decide with their heart, value harmony, can be seen as overemotional, are good at appreciating, and usually take things personally. Feeling forms conclusions in an attached and somewhat global manner, based on likes or dislikes, the impact on others, and human and aesthetic values (Reinhold 2010).

Finally, intuition suggests where it has come from or is going to. Those who prefer intuiting pay attention to their "sixth sense," to hunches and insights, and focus on what might be. Intuitives usually prefer insights, abstract information, are more interested in what is possible, focus on the big picture, are inspired and imaginative, focus on the future, value innovation, and are speculative. Intuition seeks to understand, interpret and form overall patterns of all the information that is collected and records these patterns and relationships. It speculates on possibilities, including looking into and forecasting the future. It is imaginative and conceptual (Reinhold 2010).

An individual's innate conscious orientation will be towards one of these four directions. In every person, Jung argued, there is one superior function, one auxiliary function, and one inferior function (and of course one tertiary function). For example, if thinking is one's superior or most differentiated function then feeling would be one's most undifferentiated or inferior function, or vice versa. At the same time, the remaining two functions are the so-called auxiliary functions which serve the superior function (Jung 1971). These auxiliary functions are either a secondary or a tertiary function, which have some influence on the dominant cognitive function (Jung 1971: 244–300).

Further, Jung combined the two attitudes with the four (cognitive) functions and created eight special mixed psychological types: (1) Extravert thinkers direct themselves and others according to fixed rules and principles since they are interested in reality, order and material facts. They could be scientists who discover natural laws (such as Charles Darwin), or economists who create theoretical formulations (such as Karl Marx) (Hyde, MacGuinness 82–84). As far as society and social groups are concerned, including professional groups at a general social level, law and lawyers seem to fit in the same group with economists as extravertive thinkers. Why? Because their major evaluative function is thinking and they are generally oriented towards social relationships and social conflicts as external dimensions of people's life.

(2) Introvert thinkers formulate questions and seek to understand their own being. They usually neglect the world and dwell on their own ideas (e.g. philosophers such as Ludwig Wittgenstein). In addition, there are (3) extravert feelers (e.g. chat show hosts, stars like Frank Sinatra and Madonna) and (4) introvert feelers (e.g. monks, nuns, musicians such as Chopin). We should also add to the list (5) extravert sensators, who tend to focus on external facts, are practical, hard-headed, and accept the world as it is, such as builders. Some of them might even be affable enjoyers of life (such as Casanova). Moreover, there are also (6) introvert sensators (e.g. connoisseurs, aesthetes), (7) introvert intuitivers (e.g. mystics and poets such as William Blake), and (8) extravert intuitivers (such as PR people or adventurers) (Hyde, MacGuinness, *ibid.*).

Jung was aware of the fact that in every person there predominates a certain mechanism of activity which, however, cannot get away from other mechanisms that are present in the same person, although they might be completely opposite to the dominant one. Therefore, according to Jung, there are no clear types but the notion of ideal types only points to the predominant existence of the said mechanism in a person. His methodology of creating ideal psychological types proceeded from the insights and observations he obtained while dealing with his patients. Further, these insights were appropriately reflected through the study of some previous attempts in history at creating certain types in different areas of human thought. For that reason, Jung studied the works of Schiller, Nietzsche, James and other great persons (Jung 1971). He finally analyzed all such previous attempts and tried to comprehend them by developing appropriate categories that resulted in his own theory of psychological types.

Some of Jung's followers have even gone further.

2.1.2 Empirical Post-Jungians

In addition to Jung's eight types, Isabel Myers and Katharine C. Briggs invented 16 psychological types and a special indicator (the so-called Myers-Briggs Typology Indicator – hereinafter MBTI), by which it is possible to locate certain types through psychometric measurement. Together with her mother Briggs Myers began to develop the mentioned indicator on the basis of a questionary that they composed during World War II for the purpose of indicating personal preferences which could help women working in the war industry to better use their potential (Briggs et al. 1995). The indicator was to be quite reliable since for a majority of the adults tested it demonstrated very similar results even if they took the test several times (Capraro and Capraro 2002).

What Myers and Briggs actually added to Jung's scheme of types were two additional cognitive functions, namely "judgment" and "perception", which are allegedly indispensable for better locating the types (Briggs Myers and McCaulley

1995). This was, however, strongly objected to by some "true" followers of Jung who trust his classical thought more (Jeffries 20).

In Myers' and Briggs' opinion, the two additional preferences of judgment and perception were needed in order to better address the so-called auxiliary cognitive function that was only implicitly discussed in Jung's work. The judgement-perception preference shows the way of a person's life, his or her method of dealing with the outside world. For example, those who prefer perceiving tend to live in a spontaneous, flexible way, while those who prefer judging tend to live in an organized, planned way (Baron 11). Another result of Jung ignoring the auxiliary process is the distorted description of the individual introvert types. For their extraversion introvert types need the auxiliary function, which represents their outer personality, their communication with the world, and their means of taking action. The judgement-perception preference is also allegedly indispensable for ascertaining which process is dominant. Instead of Jung's eight psychological types (introversion/extraversion x sensation/intuition/thinking/feeling), Myers and Briggs established 16 psychological types (introversion/extraversion × sensation/intuition/thinking/feeling + judgment/perception) (Myers Briggs, Myers 1995).

Furthermore, the existence and characteristics of these types were examined in numerous MBTI tests undertaken in last decades. Today the MBTI is considered to be one of the most widely used tests for measuring personal typology. It was also used for law students in order to measure their school performance in relation to their personal typology (Miller 1967). In additional to the MBTI, there have also been other upshots of Jung's psychological type theory, which followed a similar empirical approach as the MBTI.

David Keirsey and Marilyn Bates worked on developing the ancient study of temperament by Hippocrates and Plato. They divided the four temperaments into two categories (roles), each with two types (role variants). The resulting 16 types correlate with the 16 personality types described by Briggs and Myers. For that purpose Keirsey used the names suggested by Plato: Artisan, Guardian, Idealist, and Rational. These ideas ended up in a special Keirsey Temperament Sorter (KTS), which is a self-assessed personality questionnaire designed to help people better understand themselves and others (Keirsey and Marilyn 1984).

Furthermore, there was another movement that sprang out of Jungian typology: socionics. It is a theory of information processing and personality type being modification of Jung's personality type theory that uses eight psychic functions, in contradistinction to Jung's only four. It is a theory of intertype relations since the eight functions process information at varying levels and interact with the corresponding functions in other individuals. Socionics was founded in the 1970s and 1980s, primarily by the Lithuanian researcher Aušra Augustinavičiūtė. The name of this movement was derived from the word 'society' since its founder believed that each personality type has a distinct purpose in society. For that purpose the socionicists use the word 'sociotype;' they also developed a special test for measuring these intertype relations (International Institute of Socionics 2015).

Finally, to add another member to that empirical group of Jung's typology followers, I should also mention the Gray-Wheelwrights Test (GWT), also known as the Jungian Type Survey that was developed by several Jungian analysts using the original eight Jungian types or categories of type preference (Marcin 116).

All the above-mentioned (empirical) tests were, on one hand, seriously attacked in the public as being problematic for producing stereotypes by "forcing" and locking people into more or less fixed pre-established categories, denying both human agency and the significance of external factors. In such a manner, the criticism of this kind of (experimental) psychological typing continued, such tests and their results can be harmful as they could "cause and exacerbate social and individual wounds". In this way they were considered as a heresy (Marcin 104). On the other hand, they have also be seen as salvation since psychological typing has proven even in clinical practice that it has a "great potential for healing and bringing people together and has a positive role to play in creating a world in which human differences constructively complement one another" (Marcin 104).

2.1.3 Psychological Typing Between "Heresy" and "Salvation"

Since I wanted to write this book as a legal theorist or a legal philosopher, not a psychologist with a proficient knowledge of psychometrics that frankly I do not possess, in the controversy between the "faithful" and "heretic" (empiric) Post-Jungians I must side with those taking Jung as a "philosopher" of psychological types. My ambition was to discuss the types and special ideas and concepts which could be applied to a legal theory to deal with the phenomenon of law as a special social activity. Personally I do not have anything against experimental psychological typology and the above mentioned typology tests, but I can understand at best their results to be just one type of criteria for determining personal potentials of individuals, not the only ones, to be combined with other non-empiric criteria.

Hillman has suggested that the four functions in Jungian typology might be more archetypal than empirical (Hillman 1980). With this I very much agree as it seems that that was my ambition from the very beginning. Therefore, the following passage from Hillman's work, in which he was against the empirical and statistical dealing with Jung's psychological typology, is quite indicative of Jung's archetypal consideration of the types: "Then *hylikoi*, or *physis*, with its attendant ideas of matter, body, actual physical reality would be the archetypal principle in what Jung called sensation; *psychikoi*, or soul, with its attendant Jungian description of love, value, experience, relatedness, woman, salt, colour would be the archetype within and behind what Jung called feeling; *pneumatikoi*, or spirit, with its attendant descriptions in terms of light, vision, swiftness, invisibilities, timelessness, would be what Jung called intuition; and finally, not expressly distinguished in this Hellenistic triad, *nous*, logos, or *intellectus*, with its capacity for order and cognitive intelligence, would be the archetypal principle that Jung called the thinking function."

For that reason I use Jung's types as ideas, concepts or, in a Weberian sense (see below), as yardsticks against which to test certain hypotheses. I do not want to "lock" in any manner individuals into pre-existing types at face value, thus I understand the types as categories to be dynamic in the sense of being in a constant flux and interaction with internal and external influences. Only as such can they be applied in my integral theory of law, which, as it follows in the continuation, is based on dialectics or dialectic relations between the opposing types. I think this was also Jung's original idea when he embarked on his 20-year mission of studying and writing about the psychological types. If I opted for some kind of static categories there would be no dialectic understanding of their interaction either in an individual or society. I think the warnings against the rigidity of typological empiricism have a certain value when pointing in this direction.

However, in various works on the MBTI's application and results one can find useful elements even for such a philosophical discussion on the psychological types. I am sure that it is almost a commonsense that from the types' general definitions or categories, in the sense of a conceptual analysis, some more specific elements, tenets, features or facets can be extracted. Their (scientific) value is even greater if they have been empirically tested even though such testing might be too restricting upon the individual as an integral personality. These facets seem to simply be logically deduced from the general descriptions of the types and thus might be seen as their logical concretizations. This could have been done on the basis of a Weberian sociological analysis as well. Thus in the following paragraphs I am referring to a particular work from an "empirical" Post-Jungian in which the author discusses certain facets that we should associate with particular four cognitive functions.

Accordingly, for sensing as a cognitive function Quenk emphasizes that it focuses on what can be perceived by the five senses. Initially there is the (1) concrete that focuses on concrete, tangible, and literal perceptions, communications, learning styles, world view, and values. It trusts what is verifiable by the senses, and is cautious about going beyond facts. Then what is typical of sensing is the (2) realistic which prefers what is useful, has tangible benefits, and accords with common sense. It values efficiency, cost-effectiveness, conformity, and security. Furthermore, as a characteristic of sensing the (3) practical is more interested in applying ideas than in the ideas themselves and likes working with known materials and using practical, familiar methods. It prefers modest, tangible rewards over risky opportunities for greater gain. The (4) experimental as another characteristic of sensing trusts its own and other's experience as the criterion for truth and relevance and learns best from direct, hands-on-experience. It focuses more on the past and present than the future. Finally, what is typical of sensing is also the (5) traditional, which likes the continuity, security, and social affirmation provided by traditions, established institutions, and familiar methods. It is uncomfortable with fads and unconventional departures from established norms (Quenk 10).

A certain antipode to sensing is the cognitive function of intuition. According to Quenk what is firstly typical of it is the (a) abstract that focuses on concepts and abstract meanings of ideas and their interrelationships. It tends to use symbols, metaphors, and mental leaps to explain its interests and views. The next characteristic of intuition is the (b) imaginative, which values possibilities over tangibles and likes ingenuity for its own sake. It is also resourceful in dealing with new experiences and solving problems. Moreover, what is characteristic of intuition is the (c) conceptual. It likes knowledge for its own sake and focuses on the concept, not its application. It enjoys complexity and implied meanings over tangible details, and likes to take risks for large potential gains. Another characteristic of intuition is the (d) theoretical that sees relevance beyond what is tangible and trusts theory as having a reality of its own. It is future oriented and sees patterns and interrelations among abstract concepts. A final characteristic of intuition can be the (e) original that tends to value uniqueness, inventiveness, and cleverness to put meaning into everyday activities. Also it enjoys demonstrating its own originality, and believes that sameness detracts from meaning (Quenk, *ibid.*).

Furthermore, for thinking as a cognitive function what is initially typical is the (i) logical that believes that using logical analysis and hard data is the best way to make decisions, and focuses on cause and effect, pros and cons. The next characteristic of thinking is the (ii) reasonable, which uses sequential reasoning, fairness, and impartiality in actual decision making, and is confident and clear about objectives and decisions. What is also characteristic of thinking is the (iii) questioning that asks questions to understand, clarify, gain common ground, solve problems, and find flaws in its own and others' viewpoints. Thinking is also (iv) critical since it uses impersonal critiquing of ideas, situations, and procedures to arrive at truth and avoid the consequences of flawed ideas and plans. Last, but not least, it is (v) tough by means of standing firm on decisions that have been thoroughly considered and critiqued and wishing them to be implemented quickly and efficiently (Quenk 11).

Finally, according to Quenk, the feeling function bases conclusions on personal or social values with a focus on understanding and harmony. The first facet of feeling is 'empathetic' in believing that a decision's impact on people should be primary and focusing on values and relationships. The second is 'compassionate' in considering the unique and personal needs of individuals rather than objective criteria as important in decision-making. Following Quenk, 'accommodating' is the third facet. It values harmony and the incorporation of diverse viewpoints as more effective ways to gain common ground than confrontation. The fourth facet of 'accepting' uses tolerance of the other to arrive at a mutually satisfying plan or procedure and is open to a broad range of ideas and beliefs. Finally, the 'tender' facet uses gentle persuasion and a personal approach to reach an agreement (Quenk, *ibid.*).

Interestingly, Jung's division between rational and irrational cognitive functions has recently been reiterated by moral psychologist Johnatan Haidt in his The Righteous Mind (subtitled "Why Good People Interestingly Are Divided by Politics and Religion"). With respect to the psychological types Haidt makes an important distinction in particular between intuition and thinking, the first being a perceptive and thus an irrational function and the second an evaluative and rational cognitive function. Having drawn on the latest research in neuroscience, genetics, social psychology, and evolutionary modelling, he claimed that "intuitions come first, strategic reasoning second" in the sense that our moral intuitions arise automatically and almost instantaneously as being based on our biological structure. They came "long before our moral reasoning has a chance to get started, and those first intuitions tend to drive our later reasoning" (Haidt xx–xxiii). Haidt described that distinction by also using a metaphor of a rider (reasoning) riding on an elephant (intuition), in which the "rider's function is to serve the elephant" (Haidt 108).

Haidt's categorization of the cognitive functions is certainly much weaker and much less elaborated than Jung's but an important message from his book is that to some extent the gist of Jung's psychological typology has been discovered anew by modern cognitive science.

2.2 Law, Legal Practice, and Jung's Cognitive Functions

2.2.1 The Central Position of Thinking Concerning Law

In this part I try to indicate those type preferences that prevail in legal practice and law in general. As indicated before, I am not so much interested in carrying out a psychometric research and analysis by means of locating and testing individual lawyer types, but more in establishing some basic preferences that special types of persons who professionally deal with law exhibit. Needless to emphasize that such special types of legal professions have traditionally been known in society as distinct legal professionals (such as, for example, a judge, attorney, or law professor).

It is a commonsense as well as has empirically been proven that in the case of lawyers, the superior cognitive function is to a great extent thinking, being a rational function. The auxiliary functions that to some significant extent direct and determine thinking are sensation and intuition. Below, I will be focusing on their respective roles in legal thinking.

From the above-mentioned we can try to understand why there have always existed two general types of thinking (and rationality) in law. On the one hand, there is empirical rationality, in which thinking (evaluation) obtains relevant data or information (perception) mostly from sensation, by experiencing legal standards as major premises mostly through the senses, evaluating such by thinking, and making a final decision. In this context, I have already argued that such empirical rationality is typical of the way legal positivists approach the resolution of unclear[1] or hard cases. As already mentioned legal positivists are, epistemically speaking,

[1] I have borrowed the designation of "clear case" from MacCormick, who differentiated such from "unclear case" in order to eliminate the controversy between easy and hard cases as, according to him, in the contemporary conditions of extremely complex societies there are no easy cases at all (MacCormick 2005: 50–52).

empiricists, so their main sources of perception – in this case legal norms – are mostly sensory or materialistic.

On the other hand, in the framework of legal decision-making, as already mentioned in the introductory chapter of this book, there is room also for intuitive rationality, which contributes to the establishment of a new legal norm (in case of gaps in the law) or to the essential supplementation of an existing legal norm (in case it is vague). Such is applied more in unclear cases on the basis of, e.g., moral legal principles. In contradistinction to legal positivism, the epistemic approach of natural (or non-positivist) lawyers to the above-mentioned problem would be rationalist, and their main perceptive function intuitive. In such a case, thinking obtains relevant legal information from intuition because sensation cannot help much as the text of the relevant legal norm has gaps, is vague, or ambiguous – in short, unclear. In the framework of such, (introverted or 'creative') intuition as the main source of perception is determinate for the result of such decision-making.

According to Jung, thinking is the psychological function which, following its laws, brings the contents of ideation into conceptual connection with one another. It is an appreciative activity, and as such may be divided into active and passive thinking. Active thinking corresponds to the concept of direct thinking. Passive thinking can be called intuitive thinking. Jung called the capacity for direct thinking intellect, while he named the capacity for passive or undirected thinking intellectual intuition. Furthermore, he characterised directed thinking as a rational function, because it arranges the contents of ideation under concepts in accordance with a rational norm of which one is conscious. However, when it came to undirected thinking, he at first asserted that it was, in his view, an irrational function, because it arranges and judges the contents of ideation by norms of which one is not conscious and therefore cannot recognise as being in accord with reason. Subsequently, however, he had to recognise that the intuitive act of judgment accorded with reason, although it comes about in a way that appears to one as irrational (Jung 1971).

I would not find the above-said much different from what in scholastic philosophy has been understood as the division between *ratio* and *intellectus*, the former being the ability of a discursive manner of thinking, with the latter being the ability of 'direct' (i.e. intuitive) intelligence (Maritain 1951: 111). The latter corresponds to Jung's intellectual intuition (passive thinking) while the former to intellect (direct thinking). In such a manner, the dimension of thinking as a rational function can also be divided into two main groups that underline the traditional rationalist/ empiricist dilemma. While *ratio*'s perception is predominantly empiric or sensory, intellect's perception is primarily intuitive. It is due to the difference in perception that our cognition is predominantly carried out either through intuition or through the senses.

Stemming from the fact that law's traditional role has been to provide security and stability concerning social relations, it is not difficult to establish that the main cognitive function to serve that purpose is thinking. Other traditional tenets of law have been rationality, logic, analysis, predictability, impartiality, evaluation etc. All these elements that are associated with law can be ascribed to thinking, which analyses, categorises, decides, evaluates, differentiates, integrates, synthesises etc. The thinking function is not only typical of lawyers but lawyers are people who, when dealing with law, apply it as their superior rational function. It was Weber in particular who defined the law as explicitly rational and systematic. According to him, this was why the interests of the bourgeoisie to have secure and predictable goods traffic, and legal transactions thereof, led to great legal codifications. Weber emphasised that the lawyer is a professional whose activity is predominantly formal and logical (Weber 882).

It is therefore not difficult to conclude that the function of thinking is the psychological function which is superior in persons who professionally deal with law, i.e. lawyers. It is thinking that enables them to approach the situation logically by analysing (concrete) facts in an impersonal manner, and to seek objective truth that is independent of the personality and wishes of the thinker or anyone else, with this imperative especially applying to judges.

Both rational cognitive functions (thinking and feeling) are functions or processes of making an evaluation or judgement. In the framework of the thinking function, basic conclusions are made on the basis of logical analysis with a focus on objectivity and detachment.

If amongst lawyers the thinking function is the most differentiated, their least differentiated function is certainly feeling (which, according to Jung, is also rational). It is the function that evaluates according to personal values, such as, for example, affinity for one person over another because of his or her dress, smell, shoes, clothes, the way they address people or speak to them etc. Concerning the feeling function, the abovementioned five facets that are typical of thinking (i.e. logic, reasonableness, questioning, critique and toughness) can be juxtaposed with empathy, compassion, accommodation, acceptance and tenderness (Quenk, *ibid.*). If by feeling we decide according to our subjective, i.e. personal, values, then on the basis of thinking we decide by following our objective (impersonal) values, such as justice, fairness, and legal certainty. Yet lawyers are human beings and also possess feeling to a certain extent which, however, is not (or should not be) the decisive criterion for their legal decision-making if they want to uphold the values of predictability, neutrality, objectiveness etc.

Based on the above, we can establish that, given that lawyers' superior cognitive function is thinking and feeling is their inferior function, there also remain sensation and intuition as their auxiliary functions. In this connection, a former Slovenian Supreme Court judge interestingly described the atmosphere in his professional environment by explaining that, unlike in the courtroom, in his free time he was also a "human being" with all his emotions and feeling. He thereby meant that the lawyers' profession does not allow for the world of emotions, which much more affect the feeling function than thinking, to prevail in a courtroom as the main standards or criteria for legal decision-making demands "cold" reason and clear thoughts. He confessed that while in the courtroom he had to strongly adhere to the rational landscape of the lawyers' world, but when he came out he was free and lucky to enjoy the entire life of emotions and feeling (Ogrizek 2000).

What is typical of modern law is the fact that its legal proceedings are highly formalised, as reflected in the very detailed and systematically categorised rules of procedure. Moreover, substantive legal rules that are embodied in various codes of law are very abstract and general. A well-functioning legal system also tends to be systematic. All these elements such as formality, abstractness, generality and systematisation which are typical of modern law are characteristic of a very much differentiated thinking function of the human psyche. However, having taken all of this into consideration, one may ask oneself whether there is any place for feeling in the area of law, legal decision-making, and the professional life of lawyers which, as mentioned above, is also a rational function, but very much connected with and dependant on emotions and personal values. Certainly, due to it being a product of people's normative activities, law cannot be absolutely value-neutral, but to some extent at least includes the consideration of certain values such as justice, fairness, legal certainty, predictability, equality etc., by those who are engaged in the processes of creating and applying law. This entails that in law there is also room for passion, fervour and ambition in seeking the fulfilment of these values. However, in a modern legal setting, even in relation to the values that have been accepted in formal legal rules and principles as legal values, the feeling function is mainly a motivating factor behind some of these values, not a decisive criterion for the resolution of disputes concerning them. In such a manner, it is subordinate to the thinking function whose main role is to resolve disputes by logical means, thus preventing usually very emotionally affected parties from resorting to violent self-protection.

Nevertheless, one must not forget the role of the feeling function especially in those more informal settings that are complementary to formal legal proceedings. This particularly applies to alternative dispute resolution procedures (e.g. mediation, conciliation, settlement etc.). It is especially the informality of such procedures that gives the feeling function its proper role, which is expressed in several dimensions of such a "dispute", in particular when it comes to mediation. In such an informal setting, which resembles more conversation than trial, there is room for the expression of personal values, even outbursts of emotion, which might contribute to a catharsis and thereby perhaps to the resolution of a dispute, which in some areas of law (like family law) might be a better means for resolving a conflict or dispute than strictly legal means. This especially applies to those areas in which it is preferred that existing social relations continue (i.e. family relations, business relations). Hence the important role of psychologists, social workers and various kinds of therapists in alternative dispute resolution procedures as mediators who are not necessarily lawyers (Roach Anleu 124–129).

Therefore, the role of the feeling function is particularly important for some new developments in law and jurisprudence such as preventive law, ADR, procedural justice, therapeutic jurisprudence (Abadinsky 375–376), problem-solving courts, restorative justice, collaborative law, holistic law, and creative problem solving (Daicoff 169–186). According to Daicoff, such lawyers' concerns are mostly people's relationships, values, goals, needs, emotions and resources, which is more typical of the feeling function or an ethic of care. These traits, such as altruism, non-materialism or non-competitiveness promote values other than wealth maximisation and winning adversarial battles, are certainly atypical of traditional law (Daicoff 192–193). They can be important supplements to the traditional role of the thinking function in law, although they cannot simply substitute its importance.

It seems that to some extent the postmodern legal mind has shifted its attention from the modernist understanding of law as more or less a logical system of legal rules being unitary and separate from other dimensions of culture and society (Goodrich and Carlson 1998), which culminated in, e.g., Kelsen's pure theory of law founded on an isolated system of legal rules tighten together by logic and linguistics. Speaking typologically, what was typical for the modern conception of law was its predominant emphasis on rationality and the ensuing detachment of law from emotions and irrationalities. Here we need to understand that, according to Jung, feeling is a rational function but still closer to emotions, taking them much more into consideration than thinking. One example of contemporary legal theorists' increased interest in the emotions in analysing law[2] was the title of the 2015 congress of the international society for the philosophy of law and social philosophy (abbreviated to IVR): Law, Reason and Emotion, and various plenary topics that were dedicated to the role of emotions in law and legal practice (IVR 2015).

The preceding paragraphs presented the positive role of feeling that, to some extent, is important concerning the phenomenon of law. However, it needs to be emphasised that when feeling is applied with the task of resolving legal issues, rigid formalism as the manner of decision-making and justification is possible to occur. The feeling function does not possess all the nuances associated with rationality in contrast with the thinking function since thinking is a much more differentiated type of rationality than feeling when it comes to reasoning and argumentation. Since feeling is more deciding according to personal values it is more one-sided, which could also be a trait of formalism, not to mention the problem of objectivity and impartiality in relation to feeling as a mode of decision-making. Consequently, this leads us to the idea that thinking seems to be still a more appropriate and prevailing means for resolving legal disputes than feeling. I am sure that was also one of the conclusions of the above-mentioned IVR congress in 2015 by still recognizing to an important extent, however, the role of emotions in law, which seem to be greater than we have ever admitted to ourselves.

In accordance with the above, it seemed appropriate to create the following figure as regards the state of the superior, inferior and auxiliary functions of the

[2] See, e.g., the following contributions: Kwame Anthony Appiah, A Decent Respect: Honor in the Life of the Law; Ko Hasegawa, Interactive Reason in Law; Matthias Mahlmann, Mind and Rights: Neuroscience, the Critique of Reason and the Foundations of Legal Justice; Daniel Mendonca Bonnett, Rights, Reaon and Emotion: Conflict of Rights and Balancing Rights; Patricia Mindus, The Wrath of Reason and the Grace of Sentiment: Vindicating Emotion in Law; Andras Sajo, The Constitutional Domestication of Emotion (see also Sajo 2011), and Robin West, Lawful Emotions (IVR 2015: 51–61).

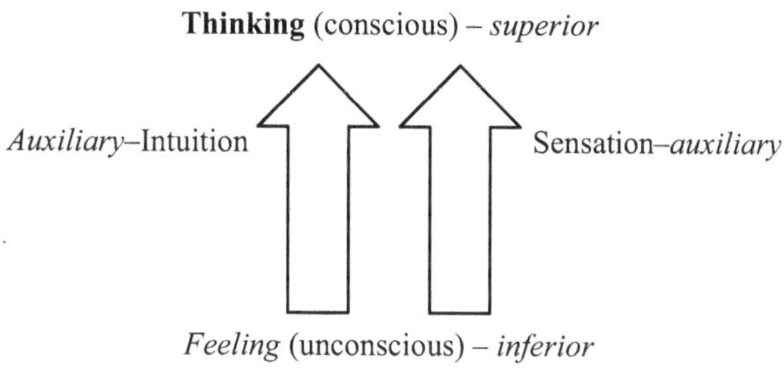

Fig. 2.2 The typological "state" of the lawyer's (most typical) psyche

lawyer's (most typical) psyche in terms of Jung's psychological type theory (Fig. 2.2).

The predominance of rationality (i.e. thinking) is certainly not only a characteristic of law, but also of certain other social activities. However, in order to find in the phenomenon of law some special characteristics which differentiate it from other social activities that also largely use thinking as their primary function, reference could be made to the classical distinction with regard to human reason between theoretical reason and practical reason as two separate systems of thinking, a distinction which is as old as Aristotle. In modern times Christian Wolf assigned ethics, economics and politics to practical philosophy, for which "action" is typical, while theoretical philosophy was to comprise ontology, psychology, cosmology, and theology (as "contemplation") (Mautner 441).

It is well known that, on one hand, theoretical reason deals with questions such as reflection on facts seeking the reasons for their existence. It refers to the understanding of the world around us by trying to find the truth, usually by experiment. Such issues are studied predominantly within the natural sciences and social sciences, which conduct research into the reasons and consequences of certain more or less objectively perceived activities (the so-called laws of nature and technical laws). In sociology there are measurements of public opinion, in psychology psychometrics, in economics statistics and other calculations which are similar to the operation of the natural and technical sciences. Theoretical thinking is thus interested in finding the truth or confirming (at least the acceptability of) certain hypotheses.

In contrast, law as a special social activity falls within the so-called normative or practical areas, which deal with imperatives. According to the mentioned classical distinction, such refers to practical rationality which takes normative issues as its starting point. These areas mainly refer to values when they evaluate and weigh reasons for a certain activity (Wallace 2009). It deals with alternatives to be selected as better (or more just) options. Such thinking can be called normative thinking.

Among the most important social rules there are legal rules which are differentiated from laws of nature and technical laws that reflect the operation of natural forces, their relations and their causes and effects. Social rules also differ from technical rules which determine the use of natural force by human beings in order to achieve certain effects, and thus regulate our relationship with nature. However, social rules regulate human relations within a society and between human beings. They call for certain conduct, demand certain respect that depends on the will and consciousness of members of a society. If such required conduct is disrespected, the society needs sanctions to be applied as a certain positive encouragement for people to obey social rules. Laws of nature do not possess such sanctions and also do not need them because of their cause and effect automatism.

However, law as a system of social norms is not the only human activity that deals with practical rationality (or practical thinking). There are also moral norms or morality, which has traditionally been an important activity that falls within the area of practical thinking. In this aspect, one possible distinction between these two activities can be made by using Kant's famous idea that law refers more to external matters of human life, while morality is more an internal issue of people.

In addition to moral norms, other social norms include customs and even other seemingly less important social rules, such as rules of grammar, sports rules, general rules of conduct etc. In comparison with such social rules, it is not difficult to establish that legal rules originate from a very organized social structure supported by various (mainly state) institutions. In the case of law and legal rules, complexity and the level of organization is much higher than in the case of other social rules. For example, the operation of morality is much more spontaneous than the operation of legal rules and legal institutions. Since global human society today includes a growing number of individuals it is becoming increasingly complex, which is also why we have ever more social and legal rules. Thus, it seems appropriate to agree with MacCormick that law is also a so-called institutional normative order (MacCormick 2007). It is certainly a product of a modern highly organized society that presupposes the existence of numerous institutions and (state) bodies that create and apply legal acts in order to resolve important social disputes. Such institutions are also a product of the historical, civilizational and cultural development of society.

2.2.2 The Sensation-Intuition Dichotomy

Having established that, according to Jungian typology, the function of the psyche that is predominantly engaged in the daily work of lawyers is thinking, and that their most inferior function is feeling, I now turn to the role of the two auxiliary functions to demonstrate their influence on the superior function. How do the auxiliary functions affect the understanding and shaping of law as a product of practical thinking? At this point, let me just repeat that sensation refers more to information we receive through our five senses and is oriented more to the external world, while intuition, as our "six sense", transmits to us the messages we receive from our inner self (when the matter concerns introvertive intuition). It focuses mainly on perceiving patterns and interrelationships. However, the fact that thinking is the superior function in the legal profession entails that thinking will dictate the goals, and sensation and intuition will only be allowed to suggest suitable means for reaching them.

When it comes to the influence of sensation on thinking, as already mentioned Jung referred to the traditional concept of *ratio* which entails that our thinking receives external information and analyses such in the framework of experimental logic by showing that certain things are causes of certain effects (Jung 1971). This is also the way in which science operates and tries to prove its discoveries, and is also the language of analysis and argumentation in law that deals with rules and principles that are written in legal codes. Not only is it the language of contemporary legal rules, but also of rhetoric, reasoning and argumentation in judicial decisions, legal logic, and of commentaries on different legal codes and acts. Accordingly, it is the language of positive law and also, to an important extent, of positive-law legal theories. Today this language as the language of instrumental rationality predominates in legal discussion.

Beside *ratio*, Jung also mentioned what has traditionally been perceived as *intelectus*. In this context he referred to intellectual intuition as a special type of thinking that obtains information from intuition (Jung 1971). We can point to the role of intuition in law by emphasising the role of various hunches and insights in the process of legal decision-making. This was particularly emphasised by the American Legal Realists, Frank ("hunches") and Hutcheson ("judgment intuitive"), as well as by Petrazycki in his concept of intuitive law. According to him, rules of intuitive law, not being limited by any normative fact, are experienced as resulting from the very nature of things – natural, just, universally valid (Petrazycki 2011). Moreover, Petrazycki equated his concept of intuitive law with the sense of justice (Motyka 28–29).

Nevertheless, today this type of language is mostly reserved for more theoretical, even philosophical, reflections on the problem of legal rules such as whether certain legal rules are just or fair in relation to various principles, and as a tool in reaching legal decisions when various insights, including moral sentiments, help us come to a just decision for example when there is a need to fill a gap in the law. In terms of contemporary law, intellectual intuition is undoubtedly subordinate to the more predictable formal language of law. Such intellectual (i.e. introvertive) intuition can also be called "creative intuition".

But this does not mean that in dealing with positive law there is no room for intuition. Quite the contrary, intuition also plays a very important role in more "instrumental" environments. The importance of intuition in law in general stems from the fact that law is mostly a "game" of language, which is composed of words, concepts and symbols. In this respect, the role of intuition is to translate such abstract language into concrete reality in order that it becomes meaningful (Briggs Myers, Myers 57–59). Thus, it is indispensable for understanding legal language which is full of concepts, abstractions and generalisations. However, in contradistinction with the previously mentioned creative intuition the intuition that is used in positive-law contexts is mainly extravertive can be called "instrumental intuition". Its role is to "navigate" or direct the lawyer-thinker through various abstract and general rules and principles of positive-law codes to his or her final legal decision.

Such instrumental intuition can to some extent be equated with the concept of (intuitive) "recognition," as the one which helps the lawyer *a priori* understand, or at least seriously "guess," whether certain facts fit a certain legal norm and can thus be subsumed under it (the so-called *Rechtsgefühl*).

This initial phase of using the so-called legal sense (or, better, legal intuition) is very important for practicing lawyers and judges in order for them to make a first "diagnosis" of the resolution of the case. This first "diagnosis" of the case, metaphorically like in medicine, very much determines the course or proceeding in which the decision-maker by means of (rational) thinking comes to a decision and then reasons as such.

Another special feature of thinking that deals with law is the fact that legal rules are predominantly expressed in the form of (mostly written) language. This is why the thinking (by means of logic, analysis, synthesis) that deals with law refers to a special human intelligence for language (Gardner 1993) which to some extent is, for example, different from the so-called mathematical-logical intelligence that deals with numbers.[3] In contradistinction with the logical-mathematical form of intelligence, the world of language is not closely connected with the concrete world as the world of concrete objects (Gardner 1993). Language is very much linked with abstraction and intuition. Moreover, legal language resulting from (rational) thinking is also quite different from the language of art when literature as its special form is concerned.[4]

Concerning the predominance of the impact of one or other auxiliary function on thinking, I differentiate between the lawyer who is more inclined to positive (i.e. sensatory or empirical) law and the lawyer who is more inclined to non-positive (intuitive) law. The more positive-law-oriented lawyer-thinker is closer to the real world of facts, practical problems and concrete relations. Here the prevailing thinking function receives information predominantly from the empiric world of sensation. In this context, instrumental intuition necessarily plays a subordinate role to the thinking-sensation combination.

Conversely, to an important extent the predominantly intuitively (in the creative way) oriented lawyer-thinker is remote from the concrete world of facts but is closer to his or her internal world of ideas. Maritain asserted that in terms of natural law the matter deals with findings from intuition by means of listening to some internal "melody" of mind (Maritain 1951: 95). Moreover, in his Preface to Metaphysics he claimed that Kant had never understood the proper role of intuition in approaching metaphysical truths (Maritain 1962: 52). That would undoubtedly be close to what Bergson understood by his concept of intuitive morality.

Recently, Mikhail in his Elements of Moral Cognition has used Noam Chomsky's (linguistic) idea of universal grammar and applied it to morality, developing the concept of innate universal moral grammar. For that reason he

[3] In my classes there has always been a majority of law students who disliked mathematics.

[4] A typical example of this is poetry in which thinking certainly has some role, although it is often subordinated to feeling.

used behavioral and neuroscientific evidence to demonstrate how ordinary adults and even younger children make sophisticated moral judgments based upon their moral intuitions. In Mikhail's opinion "the concept of a Universal Moral Grammar is a rich empirical content and is more than a mere play on words" (Mikhail 2011).

Mikhail's position on morality is very much in tune with what Jung considered perception based on introvertive intuition. A lawyer's or judge's creative intuitive function as an auxiliary function that carries hunches from the internal being to (rational) thinking is in particular important for using internal or intuitive dimensions of law such as the sense of morality, the sense of justice, the sense of social-legal issues such as equality etc. In the framework of legal decision-making – especially when it comes to hard cases like when a text is unclear, includes gaps and there are several solutions to the problem – the mentioned dimension of intuitive thinking is very important.

Based on the above, it seems that the sensation-intuition dichotomy concerning law and lawyers is not as important as the previously mentioned thinking-feeling dichotomy. This follows from the fact that with law neither intuition nor sensation stand out as an absolute type preference as was the case of thinking. However, both preferences are indispensable for dealing with law as they represent the cognitive functions of perception.

A lawyer learns positive law, including legal rules and legal principles that are incorporated in legal regulations, through their senses, and such a world of positive law is thus for them part of the world of facts that encompass them. It is the external reality that in the process of legal interpretation and deciding the lawyer must evaluate by means of the evaluative function that is represented in him or her by thinking. Certainly it is impossible to exclude from thinking other parts of the lawyer's personality which might have a certain impact on their evaluative activity. It is particularly positive law, being a starting point for his or her work, which also represents a limitation on his or her evaluation. At this point, it is clear that the less the legal standards the judge must compulsorily consider in their adjudication are envisaged in advance (i.e. more or less precisely determined in legal texts of codes or case law), the more they are free to make decisions, which makes their personality a more important factor in decision-making. Regardless of whether there are gaps in the law, a lawyer's instrumental intuition forms an integral part of his or her functioning in the framework of positive law since, without such, the understanding or recognition of legal concepts when they are faced with the facts of cases would be strongly minimised.

Given the fact that by its form positive law represents a certain objectification of prevailing social interests at a certain time and place, which can only be amended within a certain procedure that is envisaged in advance, this certainly brings security to disputable social relations. Positive law that plays an important role of a mediator between people thus represents a certain compromise or common denominator that is determined in some act or case. Creative intuition, in this respect the "subjective law" of every interpreter or judge that decides on a certain case, is in this sense only a supplement to positive law. In this context, positive law would be a form, while intuitively perceived law somewhat substantively or

Table 2.1 Classification of lawyers in various legal professions according to the sensation-intuition dichotomy

	Sensation	Intuition
Legal practice	Attorneys (litigation)	Attorneys (research & writing)
	Judges at lower courts	Judges at superior courts
	State attorneys, prosecutors	
Legal academia	Positive-law theorists	Non-positive law theorists
	Legal historians	Scholars, writers
	Professors practicing law	
Law students	Interested in positive-law courses, legal history, economics and law	Interested in non-positive law courses

materially supplements positive law, especially when it comes to various gaps in the law. However, intuitive or theoretical (non-positive) law (e.g. certain senses of justice, morality, legal sense in general, the sense of legal certainty, the sense of other legal and social values) can also play the role of a supervisor over positive law.

However, this comparison cannot serve as the basis for a general claim that when it comes to law, in terms of the auxiliary functions, intuition is more important than sensation. While in academic environments the subtleties of intuition, in the form of critical thinking, imagination, new theories etc., are very emphasized, legal practice is more focused on the "tough" way of thinking with its strong emphasis on the thinking-empirical (or sensory) dimension of the finding of facts and their more or less easy subordination to rules. This at least applies to clear cases, which in legal practice certainly predominate, at least at the lowest levels of (judicial) decision-making.

Finally, the abovementioned findings and ideas are presented below in a table that demonstrates several aspects of the probability of lawyers' type preferences in various legal professions according to their sensation-intuition dichotomy. This attempt to classify lawyers according to their perception type preferences is not crucial for the elaboration of my type theory and is of an introductory character. Still it might seem to be useful for lawyers to see what possibilities there are and their probable preferences when it comes to this aspect of the cognitive functions (Table 2.1).

Now it remains to see how lawyers are likely to differ in terms of their two types of attitudes.

2.2.3 Extraversion and Introversion in Law

It is well known that one of Jung's most important psychological discoveries was the differentiation between extraversion and introversion. The extravert is more oriented to an external environment, towards the outer world of people and objects, while the introvert is more oriented to an internal environment, towards an inner world of experiences and ideas (Jung 1971).

I have already mentioned that this type of dichotomy is not crucial for my type theory of law. Still, I have also pointed out that there is hardly any Jungian psychological typology without at least mentioning this kind of dichotomy. After all, a brief analysis of its importance for law and legal professions might prove at least interesting for one dealing with law as a social phenomenon.

Quenk determines five different criteria that are typical of the extraversion-introversion dichotomy. Extraverts are more (1) initiating, which means they tend to act as social facilitators at social gatherings. They like to introduce people, connect those with similar interests, plan and direct gatherings. They are also very (2) expressive by easily telling others their thoughts and feelings, making their interests known and readily confiding in others, and are seen as easy to get to know. Further, extraverts tend to be (3) gregarious, which means they enjoy being with others and belonging to groups. They also tend to have many acquaintances and friends and do not make a sharp distinction between friends and acquaintances. Another characteristic of extraverts is that they are (4) active in that they like direct involvement in active environments, and learn best by doing, listening, observing and speaking rather than by reading and writing. Finally, they tend to be (5) enthusiastic in that they are talkative and lively, enjoying a dynamic flow of energy in conversations; and in liking being the centre of attention and sharing who they are by telling stories (Quenk 2009).

In contradistinction with that, introverts are more (1) receiving such that they prefer to be introduced at social gatherings, dislike small talk, prefer in-depth discussions of important issues with one or two people. Further, introverts tend to be (2) contained. They like to share their thoughts and feelings with a small and select few, and are hard to get to know because their reactions are mostly internal. Moreover, they are more (3) intimate by having a limited circle of close, trusted friends, preferring to talk one-on-one to people they know well; making a sharp distinction between intimate friends and casual acquaintances. Introverts also tend to be (4) reflective as they like visual, intellectual and mental engagement, learning best by reading and writing rather than by listening and speaking. They are also more (5) quiet so they seem to be reserved and quiet but often have rich internal responses to what is going on. As they may have difficulty in describing their inner experience in words, they may not prefer speaking about them (Quenk 2009).

When it comes to the extraversion-introversion dilemma it seems that different areas of law and legal professions, also like most other professions, are broad enough to include both attitudes of people in different positions in such. To be honest, a great deal of modern law encompasses so-called positive law which in its sensory and empirical aspect is well described as a product of extraverted thinking. Moreover, in that view the law is considered to be a social activity which is intended for the resolution of practical social disputes. Although in accordance with such criteria law seems be to a product of extravert thinking to an important extent, this certainly does not say that law cannot be dealt with introvertedly and that there is no place for introverts in law. In this sense, law is similar to economic and natural sciences.

In comparison with other disciplines and sciences within the extraverted-thinking group, what separates law and lawyers from other extraverted thinkers is: (1) their special consideration of language (in its narrow sense as a system of letters, words and sentences) and thus the special importance of intuition, with their language intelligence mostly being focused on logical and analytical perspectives (that has traditionally been called *ratio*) and, to some extent, (2) their special consideration of normativity (especially justice – which has traditionally been considered, in its non-positivistic sense, as a subject-matter of intellect).

Pascal interestingly describes a situation where several types of personalities attended a dinner organised by a lady. Among them there was a talented attorney (a practicing lawyer), who represented the extraverted thinker – with the auxiliary functions of sensation (more developed in him) and intuition (less developed in him). What typified him was his great interest in externity, regulations and facts. Further, it was peculiar to him that he memorised many laws and their rules, which he could quite skilfully use in the framework of thinking when dealing with his clients' problems. His thinking was characterised by combining events and facts, searching for causes and effects, in which he could successfully conceal the existence of certain information. All in all, he was a master of practical thinking (Pascal 38).

The other possibility of the thinking function in this aspect is the introverted thinker, who is more typical of philosophers (Jung mentioned Wittgenstein) (Jung 1971). Philosophers ask questions and try to understand their own existence. They thereby neglect the external world and manage to "live" on their own ideas. Such a type can also be the case as regards law when more theoretical legal areas are at issue, for example: the theory of law, philosophy of law, or sociology of law. Thus, the mentioned dinner was also attended by a distinguished scholar, an introverted thinker, who was discussing Pre-Socratic philosophy as the main force behind Alexander the Great's conquests. In doing so he used his auxiliary functions of intuition (in developing certain philosophic ideas) and sensation (by describing pure historical events and facts) (Pascal 39).

Certainly, there can be differences among lawyers as extraverted thinkers, as well as among introverted thinkers. Extraverted legal professions are more typical of legal practice – such as attorneys, prosecutors, judges etc. The most typical extraverted thinker is an attorney. Sometimes the superior function of their psyche can even be sensation, and thinking their first auxiliary function (Baron 83–84). The most extraverted of such are certainly the so-called litigators as those who represent clients at court trials. They are brilliant in controlling the external situation of a courtroom. More introverted among attorneys are so-called researchers and writers who in their offices in law firms (i.e. in a much more introverted environment than a courtroom) write legal memoranda, in the context of which they study various laws, commentaries and theoretical materials, and write legal papers. Such legal memoranda serve their colleagues – litigators – as the (introverted) basis for (extraverted) litigation.[5]

It seems that a judge is the least extraverted profession in legal practice. In their resolution of disputes they often must be much more "scholarly" oriented than attorneys as they or she also need to study various theoretical treatises in order to learn (and improve the knowledge of) tradition, history, rationale and other "logic" that usually lie behind a certain law that is to be applied. While attorneys in particular listen to their (extraverted) clients' interests, in addition to legal texts judges to a greater extent than attorneys must listen to their internal (or introverted) legal sense and the sense of justice. However, there is also a number of extraverted judges who are more successful in conducting trials than introverted judges. Introverted judges tend to be more scholarly-oriented: they are either perfect legal writers of (theoretical) legal treatises, commentaries on certain laws, or beside their main profession they are also engaged in teaching as law professors. However, in general judges still act in the framework of legal practice so the main framework of their environment is extraverted thinking, which in one way or another mainly deals with positive law. Further, the work environment of lower court judges is more extraverted (i.e. public hearings and trials; less time for studying cases in their offices) than the work environment of superior court judges which is more introverted (i.e. deciding in panels; more time for studying cases in their offices).

In legal academia, the general environment is generally theoretical, which means it is introverted. Although in such a milieu the starting point of introverted thinking is usually some existing legal text, a legal theorist often evaluates this in view of certain (internal) ideas, values and concepts such as fairness, justice, equality, legal certainty, consistency, coherence etc. However, also in legal academia there is room for extraversion. Those who are more extraverted are better teachers than introverts as they get along better with an extraverted environment such as a lecture room. Extraverts among legal theorists are also better organisers than introverts, better fund-raising people, and better at keeping contacts with their colleagues than introverts. Conversely, introvert legal professors tend to be better researchers, writers and scholars.

When law students are concerned, more extraverted students would prefer oral exams to written ones, and vice versa. In general the legal academic environment is more theoretical than legal practice so it is a better "natural" environment for introverted intuitive thinkers than legal practice in which extraverted sensatory thinkers can catch up to their introverted counterparts (Randal 2010).

In connection with theory, Jung cautioned against the danger of a thinker who is very intuitively-oriented as his theories could be too speculative or somewhat in the air if they are not firmly grounded on facts. The same was, however, although in different words, asserted by Kant when explaining that if concepts (or theories)

[5] Modern, especially North American, law firms have taken this difference into consideration very seriously. Such a distinction between more extraverted and introverted profiles would generally apply to prosecutors as well.

without facts are empty then facts without concepts (or theories) are blind. According to Schneider, the same meaning as experiment has for the natural sciences example has for "spiritual" sciences (Schneider 39).

However, in the event of a factually (or empirically) oriented scientist, there is a danger that, given all the facts that he or she deals with, there would be too little abstraction, which means that even if we can see in front of us numerous trees (facts) there is still the possibility that we are missing the concept or idea of a forest. Jung thus meant that both aspects of thinking (i.e. facts and theories) must be properly taken into consideration, and that theory and practice indeed need each other inseparably.

As indicated, it generally seems that, when seen from its practical aspect, the law is predominantly engaged in resolving disputes that relate to the external sphere of people's lives. Thus, law is in particular a practical activity for which people's extraverted orientation is typical since in the case of social disputes, legal rules and legal procedures, a person's psychic energy flows outward to the external world of facts that the lawyer defines and evaluates on the basis of legal rules, in which his or her main auxiliary psychic function is sensation, as the ability to perceive (external) facts and (external) legal rules. But, as with any thinking, at least to some extent, what also matters for the lawyer is his or her intuition that plays a (subordinate) role in relation to thinking and sensation. Nevertheless, it helps the lawyer find creative (or just) solutions that must again be submitted to a "rational experiment"[6] that is carried out by the thinking and sensation functions. This entails that, even for an intuitively reached decision, the judge must provide (thought out) reasons that are presented in the reasoning of the decision, which are submitted to the (external) public for evaluation.

The general framework of legal practice is, again, extraverted thinking-sensation activity. However, one can also deal with law theoretically in the sense of a theoretical analysis of legal practice, the development of new legal theories, or even when discussing law in terms of legal philosophy. In such a situation, the lawyer who thinks theoretically would think in particular as an introvert, meaning that the current of energy flows into his or her internal world when they evaluate facts and develop new theoretical approaches. In such activity, the more they leave the facts behind the less they are dependent on their sensatory (empirical) function, by using their intuition that enables certain insights which, however, must still be exposed to empirical reality if one is to arrive at a productive idea or concept.

As I have established previously concerning lawyers' attitudes in general, there is also not much difference between introversion and extraversion. Introverted lawyers, who are more interested in ideas and concepts, are frequently found in legal academia or in research-oriented positions in legal practice (e.g. as corporate lawyers, judges at superior courts), whereas extraverted lawyers, who are better in action, more often appear in legal practice as litigating attorneys or judges of lower

[6] Karl Popper called it "rational reconstruction" (Popper 8). The term rational reconstruction was subsequently adopted by the theory of legal argumentation (Feteris 10).

Table 2.2 Classification of lawyers in various legal professions according to the extraversion-introversion dichotomy

	Extraversion	Introversion
Legal practice	Litigating attorneys	Researching & writing attorneys
	Lower court judges (public hearings, trials)	Lawyers in public administration
		Superior court judges (deciding in panels)
Legal academia	Organisers, leaders	Writers
	Teachers	Scholars
Law students	Best performance at oral exams	Best performance at written exams

courts. This is also supported by empirical research (Randal 2010). In addition, Daicoff claimed that US lawyers are slightly more likely to be introverts than extroverts (Daicoff 2004). However, amongst judges there seem to be more extraverts than introverts (Randal 2010).

In relation to the extraversion-introversion dichotomy concerning lawyers and the law, I complete this chapter with the following table in which I tend to classify lawyers in various legal professions according to their extraversion-introversion preferences (Table 2.2).

At the beginning of this book I wrote that my interest in Jung's two attitudes (extraversion and introversion) was marginal for the development of my type theory of law. Perhaps this is so because as such a theory itself is a product of more introvertive than extravertive activity. But then when developed it is extravertively presented in a book or in the framework of a lecture. In my opinion this more or less concerns a scholar's attitude with respect to his or her creative process and product. Again it can also be seen as an interestingly elaborated (introvertive) theory of a predominantly extravertive profession. In one way or another this attitudinal dichotomy seems to be more interesting and important when it comes to differences among various legal professions – both between practical and theoretical as well as within practical ones. As this was not my major concern in this book be it enough what I presented above as a sort of general introduction or a short glimpse into the attitude dynamic concerning the legal professions.

However, the cognitive functions were much more interesting for my theory in this book as, in contradistinction with the attitudes that show the direction of our activities, the functions point to broader substantive areas of ideas or archetypes in us and society.

From this micro "landscape" of type preferences within the modern legal professions as a whole let us look for a moment more broadly and try to discuss the type preferences and their differences at a macro level, in the frame of comparative law constituting the legal "geography" of the world.

Here I slowly develop my perspective on typology from merely an individual to a social typology that is originally and crucially based on individual psychology.

2.3 A Comparative-Law Perspective

From the Jungian psychological types that primarily refer to individuals and those particular elements of such types that apply to individual lawyers as indicated above, it is perhaps possible to take a step forward from such individuals' characteristics to at least outline some characteristics of the social groups (constituting particular cultures) to which these individuals belong.

Although law in a global sense has some common characteristics, as referred to above, it is so intertwined with the general culture and civilization in which it originates. We usually assert that it is very hard to arrive at a universal concept of law because it is so strongly subject to the place and time in which it is created and applied. While this is not to deny that specific typological characteristics do prevail in different cultures. Some cultures and societies are more thinking cultures and more technically-oriented, whereas others are more feeling-oriented and more "musical". In some cultures people cherish sensation and are strongly oriented towards the world, while in some cultures they value intuition more and are more mystical. Not only individuals but also ethnic groups and even nations with their collective typology contribute their share to the variety of perspectives and evaluations in the world (Pascal 17, 22).

Therefore, the above presented general pattern of psychological typology pertaining to law and lawyers needs to be readjusted by means of considering specific patterns, or at least by taking specific influences on the general pattern into consideration, when we deal with law in terms of comparative-law perspectives. These specific influences seek to either modify the general pattern in one direction or another, influence it insignificantly, or even leave it untouched.

This contributes to the fact that, despite the general common denominator on the globe of the prevailing (extravert) practical rational structure of contemporary law which has been more or less established in various contemporary legal cultures, lawyers, law and legal systems certainly differ in greater or smaller details when we go from one country to another and meet lawyers and law with certain peculiarities. Finally, such partial differences in the law and legal systems of certain territories are undoubtedly reflected in general differences between lawyers from different parts of the world.

In comparative-law theory there are three predominant world legal families or groups of legal systems, i.e. (1) the European Continental (also Romano-Germanic) legal system; (2) the Anglo-American (common law) legal system; and (3) religious and traditional legal systems (Zweigert and Kötz 1998; David and Grasmann 1988). When it comes to understanding law in the light of either the creation or application of such, it seems that not only do historical and geographical differences between the mentioned world legal systems matter, but so too are differences related to various elements in terms of the different psychological typologies of such systems. The partially different legal systems are also reflections of the partially different psychological typologies of the people who create and apply law in such legal systems. Thus, it is interesting to see how the above described general or ideal typological model or pattern concerning law, which is primarily based on the thinking cognitive function, is importantly supplemented and adjusted in various world legal systems. These psychological-typological or psychoanalytic characteristics of distinct areas or legal cultures would fall within the so-named 'meta-legal elements' as one of the criteria for creating specific legal families of the world (David, Grasmann 71–72).

As I already said I do not base my findings on empirical data concerning psychological typology, but instead analyze in an abstract and theoretical manner certain traditional differences between these world legal systems through the prism of psychological typology. I am aware that the differences as regards psychological typology relating to law that I am presenting here are somewhat simplified and relative. They more concern some prevailing or predominant elements of differences between these systems that draw no strict borderlines between them.

What is typical of the traditional European Continental legal system (hereinafter referred to as the "civil law system") is an abstract and systematic way of legal thinking, whereas the traditional Anglo-American legal system (hereinafter referred as the "common law system") has included more pragmatic and casuistic elements than the civil law system. Below I analyse certain typological elements in these systems according to the already presented criteria of general typological characteristics established by Quenk (2009). In the next paragraph I repeat some of these general typological characteristics that will be important for the analysis.

According to Quenk, it is the cognitive function of intuition that refers to abstract, conceptual, and theoretical elements. By "abstract" what is meant is its "focus on concepts and abstract meanings of ideas and their interrelationships". The abstract "uses symbols, metaphors, and mental leaps to explain their interests and views." By "conceptual" Quenk understands focusing on concepts, not their application, and by "theoretical" seeing relevance beyond what is tangible and trusting theory as having a reality of its own, as well as seeing patterns and interrelationships among abstract concepts. However, following Quenk, when it comes to the cognitive function of sensation, amongst others, the following facets are also typical of it: the concrete, the practical, and the experimental. The "concrete" "focuses on concrete, tangible, and literal perceptions, communications, learning styles, world view, and values." It "trusts what is verifiable by the senses, and is cautious about going beyond facts." The "practical" is "more interested in applying ideas than in the ideas themselves and likes working with known materials using practical, familiar methods". Moreover, the "experimental" "trusts its own and others' experience as the criterion for truth and relevance and learns best from direct, hands-on experience" (Quenk 10).

The predominant legal source in the civil law system has traditionally been statute law with its abstract and general legal rules. Such legal rules are abstract in the way they tend to envisage in advance situations in which they are to apply and thus serve legal predictability, trust in the law, and legal certainty. In statutes as codifications legal rules are general in that they refer to an undefined group of people, thereby ensuring legal equality and impartiality. On the contrary, court judgments as traditionally the main legal sources in the common law legal system are much more specific than statutes as their legal rules (in the form of *rationes decidendi*) are more tailored to (material) facts and thus to the concrete. This points to the fact that, according to the abstract/concrete dichotomy, the traditional civil-law system seems to be more abstract than the common-law system and, in such a manner, it seems that the former has been more influenced by intuition and the latter by sensation.

Moreover, the civil-law system has traditionally been more conceptual with its emphasis on legal concepts and their importance through the predominance of substantive law. However, in this sense the common-law system has been more practical with its greater emphasis on procedure and procedural law, which is not so preoccupied with legal concepts as are applied in the event of substantive law and the civil-law system.

Further, in the civil-law system the most prominent legal professional has been the legal professor, whereas in the common-law system it is the judge. This addresses the second facet of the sensation/intuition dichotomy, namely experimental versus theoretical. It follows from this that the traditional common law has put at the apex of legal professions a practitioner from the experimental world, while a theorist from the academic world is at the pinnacle of the civil-law system. This also speaks in favour of the sensational element in the event of the common-law system versus the intuitive element in the event of the civil-law world.

In addition, legal education in the civil-law system has traditionally been provided at universities, while in the common-law world young lawyers have primarily been taught at bars and by practicing lawyers. This also confirms the abovementioned difference between the intuitive (also theoretical) and the sensory (also practical) approach when it comes to major variations between the civil-law and common-law systems. However, such a difference only supplements the dominant cognitive pattern in modern law that prevails in both of the abovementioned legal systems, which is primarily focused on the thinking and judging cognitive functions.

The third group of world or great legal systems to be analysed and compared with the previous two, in terms of their typological characteristics, is the group of traditional and religious legal systems, which is by no means a coherent and uniform group of such systems. In fact, it is impossible to assert that in countries in which these traditional and religious legal systems exist these are the only legal systems in these countries. In addition to traditional and religious legal systems, almost all of these countries have developed their national legal systems which are close to either the civil-law system or common-law system depending on historical influences of one system or the other in those countries. Except for certain countries of an Islamic tradition, in such countries these traditional and religious laws are mostly only applied to limited areas of law (e.g. family law, inheritance law, some other parts of civil, and mostly private, law) (Zweigert and Kötz 1998).

What then are the biggest typological differences between the civil-law system and the common-law system on one hand and the group of traditional and religious legal systems on the other?

If civil-law and common-law systems have been strongly modernised by historical development, traditional and religious legal systems have preserved much of their law's premodern content and appearance. According to Perenič, a Slovene legal philosopher, among the main characteristics of modern law there are rationality, generality, abstractness, formality and systemisation, autonomy (Perenič 1981). This corresponds strongly to Weber's distinction between modern and premodern law (Weber 641–900). This also supports the thesis of the predominance of the thinking cognitive function in modern law in contradistinction with premodern ages, when there was a greater emphasis on other cognitive functions.

What is typical of this third group of legal systems, be they the religious laws of Islam, traditional Hindu law, traditional Chinese and Japanese laws, or traditional legal customs of Africa, is the greater connection of the formal appearance of such law with its inner life (e.g. with natural law, morals and customs). Such law not only follows from codified or simply written legal customs or religious prescriptions but also from some inner perceptions also having legal content by people who interpret and apply such law. Regarding this, one is necessarily reminded of Weber's description of the role of irrationality in premodern law, in either its formal variant (as "lawmaking or lawfinding which cannot be controlled by the intellect, for instance when recourse is had to oracles or substitutes therefor") or substantive variant (according to which, "decision is influenced by concrete factors of the particular case as evaluated upon an ethical, emotional, or political basis rather than by general norms") (Weber 656).

Thus, in these traditional and religious systems of law legal rules are still very connected with moral rules and very often with still unwritten customs that pass from generation to generation. As mentioned, such a type of law is closer to some kind of archaic law which has generally been surpassed in the process of modern development. Certainly there is a question of the extent to which such archaic legal rules can still be appropriate, on a daily basis, for today's complex and complicated world. However, history has shown that such "intuitive law", thereby taking the inner laws of morals, religion, ethics, justice etc. into consideration, will always remain an alternative to the vast predominance of contemporary positive law when it deviates too much from the substantive demands of justice, morals and ethics.

Based on the above, there is no difficulty in establishing that these traditional and religious legal environments have retained a strong connection with the cognitive function of intuition as one of the irrational cognitive functions. However, there is a difference with the role of intuition in the event of its above described role in the traditional development of the civil-law system. When it comes to traditional and religious legal systems, as well as concerning archaic law, intuition seemed to be the dominant and prevailing cognitive function, and thus an independent function, whereas regarding especially the modern civil-law system intuition has been auxiliary to and dependent on the dominant cognitive function of thinking. This strong connection of law with intuition in premodern law follows, for example, from the role of judgment by ordeal as the prevailing type of legal process up to the thirteenth century, when it was abolished (Robinson, Fergus, Gordon: 10-10-11, 27–28, 36, 115, 129, 131, 135).

Moreover, when trying to differentiate the (modern) civil-law and common-law systems from the (premodern) traditional and religious legal systems, one should not forget the role of the cognitive function of feeling in legal systems that have preserved some elements of archaic law. Let us just remind that among the main facets of feeling Quenk listed empathy, compassion, accommodation and acceptance. Otherwise, she described feeling as the cognitive function which bases conclusions on personal or social values with a focus on understanding and harmony (Quenk 11). Concerning this, it is necessary to bear in mind the fact that some recent approaches to dispute resolution that are an alternative to formal judicial proceedings have been taken from certain traditional elements of Chinese and Japanese law, as well as African legal customs. It is from these systems and the role of feeling in such concerning, for example, the settlement of disputes that anthropologists have sought solutions in the development of alternative dispute resolution (ADR) (Roach Anleu 2000). Further, it seems that the feeling cognitive function also finds its place in the recent development of the duty of care approach and therapeutic jurisprudence (Daicoff 2004), ethics in law, and similar movements which try to give some alternatives to the predominance of the thinking function in contemporary law.

Lastly, it should be recognised that the typological differences between the legal systems presented above, within the structure of comparative law theory, have been somewhat abstracted and generalised. Today we must consider the fact that contemporary law has been globalised, that the traditional differences between the mentioned systems have been blurred due to the exchange of information and the constant moving of people around the globe. However, it has to be admitted that today some basic tenets have still been preserved but the differences are not as great as they were traditionally (Fig. 2.3).

Moreover, it seems that certain types of law based on the psychological typology have not only been established geographically around the world, which finds expression in the framework of comparative law, but also historically, to which I refer in the next chapter. This is an attempt to present a psychoanalytic-jurisprudential interpretation of the historical development of law. We will see how different historical models of law and their legal institutions have been influenced by certain psychological types that were predominant in a certain epoch.

In this context psychological types are compared with sociological types like the ones developed by Max Weber. In such a manner we will see that there is a great resemblance between what Jung and Weber did in their respective scientific fields. To some extent, however, far from being aware of it, Weber has translated Jung from his individual psychological into a social or collective level of typology. Jung did consider the possibility of his psychological typology being collective but did not elaborate upon it extensively. That is, however, crucial for my type theory of law that is not only based on individual but also collective typology, as law is mostly a social and thus collective phenomenon, in which individuals participate.

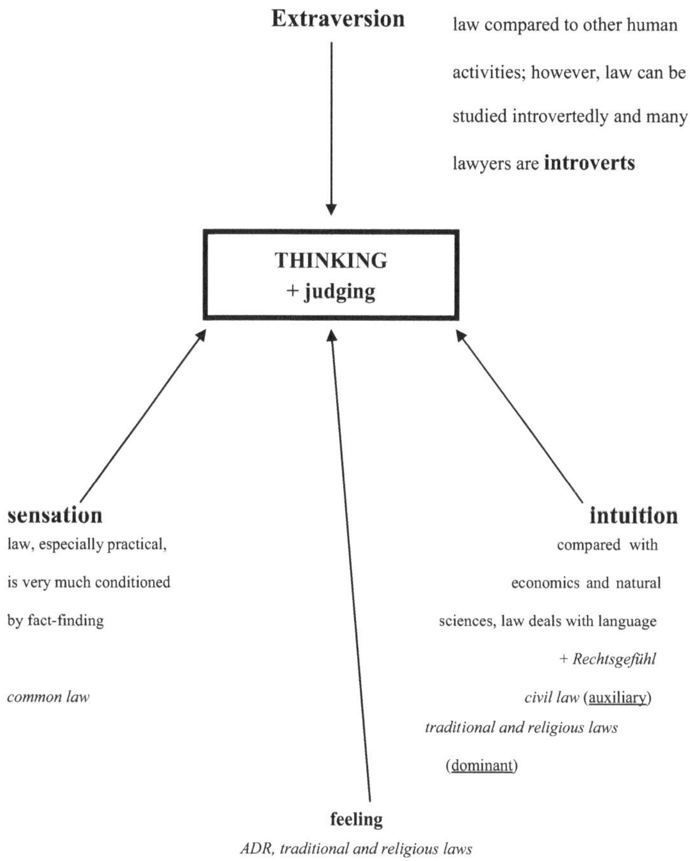

Fig. 2.3 A quick reference to the relevance of various psychological types in the global legal world

References

Abadinsky, H. (2003). *Law & justice: An introduction to the American legal system.* Englewood Cliffs: Prentice Hall.
Baron, R. (1998). *What type am I?* London: Penguine Books.
Briggs Myers, I., & McCaulley, M. (1995). *Manual: A guide to the development and use of the Myers-Briggs type indicator*. Palo Alto: Consulting Psychologists Press.
Briggs Myers, I., & Myers, P. B. (1995). *Gifts differing*. Mountain View: Davis-Black Publishing.
Capraro, R. M., & Capraro, M. M. (2002). *Educational and psychological measurement, Myers-Briggs type indicator score realibility across: Studies a meta-analytic realibility generalization study*. New York: SAGE Publications.

Daicoff, S. S. (2004). *Lawyer, know thyself.* Washington, DC: American Psychological Association.
David, R., & Grasmann, G. (1988). *Einführung in Die Großen Rechtssysteme Der Gegenwart.*
Feteris, E. (1999). *Fundamentals of legal argumentation.* Dordrecht: Kluwer Academic Publishers.
Gardner, H. (1993). *Multiple intelligences: The theory in practice.* New York: Basic Books.
Goodrich, P., & Carlson, D. G. (1998). *Law and the postmodern mind: Essays on psychoanalysis and jurisprudence (Law, modernity, and violence).* Ann Arbor: University of Michigan Press.
Haidt, J. (2013). *The righteous mind: Why good people are divided by politics and religion.* New York: Vintage Books.
Hillman, J. (1980). *Egalitarian typologies versus the perception of the unique.* Dallas: Tex. Spring.
Hyde, M., & MacGuinness, M. (1999). *Introducing Jung.* Cambridge: Icon Books.
International Institute of Socionics. (2015). Http://socionic.info/en/esocjur.html#top. Accessed 7 Oct 2015.
Internationale Vereinigung für Rechts- und Sozialphilosophie (IVR). (2015). *Law, reason and emotion*, 27 July–1 August 2015, Washington, DC, USA.
James, W. (1911). *Pragmatism.* London: Longmans.
Jeffries, W. C. (2004). *True to type.* Norfolk: Hampton Roads Publishing Co.
Jung, C. G. (1971). *Psychological types.* London: Routledge.
Keirsey, D., & Marilyn, B. (1984). *Please understand me: Temperament, character, intelligence.* Del Mar: Prometheus Nemesis Book Co.
MacCormick, N. (2005). *Rhetoric and the rule of law.* Oxford: Oxford University Press.
MacCormick, N. (2007). *Institutions of law.* Oxford: Oxford University Press.
Marcin, R. B. (1992). Psychological type theory in the legal profession. *24 U Toledo L Rev, 103,* 103–119.
Maritain, J. (1951). *Man and the state.* Chicago: The University of Chicago Press.
Maritain, J. (1962). *A preface to metaphysics.* New York: The New American Library.
Mautner, T. (Ed.). (2000). *The Penguin dictionary of philosophy.* London/Victoria/Toronto/New Delhi/Auckland/Johannesburg: Penguin.
Mikhail, J. (2011). *Elements of moral cognition: Rawl's linguistic analogy and the cognitive science of moral and legal judgment.* Cambridge: Cambridge University Press.
Miller, P. V. (1967). *The contribution of noncognitive variables to the prediction of student performance in law school.* Philadelphia: University of Pennsylvania.
Motyka, K. (2007). *Leon Petrazycki Challenge to Legal Orthodoxy.* Cracow: 23rd IVR World Congress.
Ogrizek, D. (2000). Sodnikov pogled na jezik (in pravo) [A Judge's View on the Language (and Law)]. *Podjetje in delo, XXVIII*(6–7), 1078–1085.
Pascal, E. (1994). *Jung to live by.* London: Souvenir Press.
Perenič, A. (1981). *Relativna samostojnost prava* [Law's relative independence]. Ljubljana: DDU Univerzum.
Petrazycki, L. (2011). *Law and morality.* New Brunswick: Transaction Publishers.
Popper, K. (1992). *The logic of scientific discovery.* London/New York: Routledge.
Quenk, N. (2009). *Essentials of Myers-Briggs type indicator assessment.* Hoboken: Wiley.
Randal, V. (2010). *Thinking like a lawyer.* http://academic.udayton.edu/legaled/online/study/mbti00a.htm#N_17_. Accessed 5 Jan 2010.
Reinhold, Ross. (2010). Personality pathways. Exploring personality types & its applications. http://www.personalitypathways.com/type_inventory.html. Accessed 5 January 2010.
Roach Anleu, S. (2000). *Law and social change.* London: SAGE Publications.
Robinson, O. F., Fergus, D. T., & Gordon, W. M. (2000). *European legal history.* London: Butterworths.
Sajo, A. (2011). *Constitutional sentiments.* New Haven/London: Yale University Press.

Schneider, E. (1991). *Logik für Juristen: Die Grundlagen der Denklehre und der Rechtsanwendung*. München: Verlag Franz Valhen.
Wallace, R. J. (2009). *Practical reason. Stanford encyclopedia of philosophy*, http://plato.stanford.edu/entries/practical-reason/. Accessed 17 June 2009.
Weber, M. (1978). *Economy and society*. Berkeley: University of California Press.
Zweigert, K., & Kötz, H. (1998). *Introduction to comparative law*. Oxford: Clarendon.

Chapter 3
Historical Types of Law

Abstract In a similar manner to the case of comparative law, I discuss the role of psychological typology in terms of legal history in the course of which different type models of law have been established depending on a particular psychological typology that was predominant at a certain time. These historical types express how the cognitive functions of individuals have contributed to law creation and application in history. These Jungian individual psychological typologies can be translated into collective psychological typologies, as previously done by Weber. On the basis of cognitive functions (intuition, sensation, thinking, and feeling) being collectively predominant at a certain time I have developed general and specific historical types of law such as religious law (mystical and theological), traditional law (imperial and customary), logical law (casuistic and systematic) and harmonious law.

Keywords Legal history • Cognitive functions • Weber • Collective typology • Religious law • Traditional law • Logical law • Harmonious law

When dealing with specific types, we should define what we mean by the term 'type' at the outset. Thus what I understand as a specific type is a "hypothetical construct that involves the theoretical enumeration of all the possible characteristics against which empirical material may be compared" (Roach Anleu 22). The same would refer to the types of law. The typology that is developed originates from Weber's types but, to some extent, is further developed and even modified in relation to his types. Moreover, this kind of typology has been constructed on the basis of Jung's psychological typology. Jung, and post-Jungians with their development of psychological typology, helped to interpret and extend Weber's types of law. Jung must surely have been aware of Weber, especially the Protestant Ethic thesis, but he never discussed him, while Weber did not live to see Jung's psychological types emerge (Walker 69). As in the case of Weber, the empirical material for testing the types of law has been taken from legal history. So these types of law could also be called historical types of law.

M. Novak, *The Type Theory of Law*, SpringerBriefs in Law,
DOI 10.1007/978-3-319-30643-8_3

3.1 Weber's Types of Law

One of the most important parts of Max Weber's work on law was certainly his types of law that he developed in Chapter 8 of his posthumously published book Economy and Society, which he entitled 'Economy and Law' and subtitled 'Sociology of Law'. In addition to being a classical work in legal sociology, this Weberian analysis is also an excellent study in legal history.[1] The gist of this sociological-historical work on law was in emphasizing the distinction between pre-modern and modern law, in which Weber differentiated between four types of law.

First, the charismatic revelation of law associated with the legal prophets (Weber 882) was, in Weber's opinion, of an irrational-formal character since those who "created" and "applied" the law used means that were not controlled by reason, e.g. they based their decisions on oracles or divine revelations (Weber 656). What could be added to such a type of law was, according to Weber, the irrational manner of judgments based on ordeals, the drawing of lots, duels, the swearing of an oath, sworn assistants, as well as on a sense of justice that was, in Weber's opinion, of an emotional character.[2] Moreover, Weber added jury trials to the above mentioned list.

What was important for such a conception of law was the role of elders in the society who knew the relevant sacred rites. Most often, the elders included magicians, prophets and magi. As charismatic persons these were allegedly capable of discovering, not creating, laws through revelation. It was typical of their magical techniques that they used rites which were very highly formalized. Such persons, for example, reported to their community that the divine authority required for a certain dispute to be resolved in one way or another, in the context of which they usually "received" the higher message while in a state of ecstasy or through a dream (Weber 758–775).

Secondly, Weber developed a special type of law for empirical law creation and a judiciary that was carried out by legal *honoratiores*, which he termed the rational-substantive. What is typical of this type of law is that deciding on a legal problem is not affected by norms that are created on the basis of the logical rationalisation of abstract interpretations of certain meanings, but by ethical imperatives and utilitarian as well as pragmatic rules and political maxims (Weber 657). Following Weber, such a type of law mostly developed during the time of the Roman Empire, when practically and empirically educated lawyers in particular created the special profession of the lawyer. They, however, developed a casuistic law (Lat. *casus* – legal case) which is unsystematic and thus not typical of the modern age. Weber highlighted many similarities between this type of law and the education of lawyers

[1] Weber studied law during the height of German historical jurisprudence and then taught commercial law and legal history at the University of Berlin (Roach Anleu 21).

[2] Jung would assert that such a sense of justice is conditioned much more by the role of intuition than emotions.

by various legal practitioners (particularly judges and attorneys) in Anglo-American legal systems. Such lawyers have traditionally been oriented to practical law and casuistry and for a long time declined legal codification (Weber 784–802). Even today Anglo-American law is codified to a lesser extent than European Continental law.

The third type of law was, in Weber's opinion, the law which was created and applied by great empires and theocratic authorities (Weber 882). In his opinion it is irrationally-substantive as it concerns deciding what is mostly affected by the concrete factors of a specific case which are evaluated on the basis of ethnic, emotional, and political foundations rather than on the basis of general legal norms (Weber 656). Here Weber pointed to the transition from charismatic law to a law that was based on power *(imperium)*, which occurred at the time of the partial secularization of tribal society at the end of the Roman Empire and which was strongly conditioned by the military circumstances present at the time of the Migration Period. It concerned the conscious creation of legal rules on the basis of commands issued by military chieftains or a consensus reached inside the community. The central position was no longer given to charismatic revelation of law but to military commands. Thus the military organisation of society played a very important role in the secularisation of the law, which was also to some extent connected with the patrimonialisation of the law.[3]

Furthermore, the theocratic element in such a type of law signified the power of priests as the organised guardians of law, something which was especially reflected in the increasing importance of canon law. Certainly, in such a respect the patrimonial and theocratic powers were limited by the traditional law while canon law played an important role in development of the legal system towards rationality. Despite the fact that such a system could still, to some extent, be considered as rational in terms of the application of certain principles, the matter did not concern rationality in its instrumental meaning and logical in the formal sense, but rationality more in the direction of applying certain substantive principles of social justice, or of political, utilitarian or ethical content. Such law, particularly in its patrimonial version for resolving disputes, often used discretion and considered vested privileges as some kind of a gift of grace. Such an informal patrimonial administration reached its peak when the secular ruler put himself in the service of positivistic religious interests that exceeded mere ritual frameworks (Weber 809–859).

Fourthly, and finally according to Weber, the systematic enactment of law and the professional carrying out of the judicial function by persons having a formal legal education (Weber, 882) is part of rational-formal law, which concerns a professional, legalistic and abstract approach to law in the modern sense. What is, in his opinion, typical of this last type of law is the application of an abstract method

[3] 'Patrimonial' signifies "father-like" and sometimes refers to the seizing of all three branches of power within a certain territory by the local feudal lord, which was typical of the beginning of the Middle Ages.

that uses the logical interpretation of meaning and systematizes existing legal rules into a complex and coherent system of abstract legal rules (Weber 657). Following Weber, this occurred due to the existence of the enlightened absolutist emperor, who, with the aid of his state apparatus composed of university educated lawyers trained in the spirit of the reception of Roman law, managed to build a uniform state power. The natural consequences of such a direction to law were the great legal codifications of the nineteenth century (Weber 848–859).

Weber opined that the history of law has continued and evolved in the following manner: firstly, there were primitive legal procedures in connection with a combination of magically conditioned formalism and irrationality and in which revelation played an important role. Then, an explicitly specialized legalistic and rationally-logical approach ensued and that was occasionally combined with theocratic or patrimonial informal complacency. Finally, a genuine logical sublimation and the deductive approach with the development of rational techniques in legal procedures followed (Weber 882).

In the continuation of this chapter we will see how this Weberian concept of types of law can be understood through the prism of Jung's psychological typology. However, what follow are suggestions for modifications and extensions of Weber's types.

3.2 The Weberian and Jungian Types Compared

The general relations between Weber's sociology and Jung's psychology have been considered by Walker (2012). In Walker's opinion what brings Weber and Jung together is actually sociological theory. He contends that Jung's psychology is sociologically coherent when seen in the light of sociology's major theoretical traditions, which entails that it makes sense to sociologists when seen in the light of Weber's sociology. He also asserts that Weber's historical sociology comes quite close to Jung's cultural history of the psyche. Walker further suggests that sociology should acknowledge Jung in order to orient new enquires, as well as for reflexive analysis of certain sociological debates (Walker 52–53). This is precisely my intention in this chapter: to reflect upon Weber's sociology of law on the basis of the Jungian psychological types as well as modify and extend the former on the basis of the latter. Upon analyzing how specific combinations of the dominant-auxiliary functions' relation determines certain types of law, the analysis which follows will focus on developing types of persons dealing with the law or legal professionals. In any given structural and cultural situation, certain personality types will predominate and tend to shape their structural and cultural settings around them.

Both authors would certainly agree that in the course of social development, the evolution from pre-modern to modern law to some extent corresponds to the progress from the important role of irrationality in law to the subsequent importance of rationality. Take Weber's development from irrational pre-modern types of law to those modern based on rationality (both in the formal and substantive versions) or Jung's comparison between the irrational (intuition, sensation) and rational (thinking, feeling) cognitive functions: both of them support the idea of a certain progress or at least an important change in people's cognition over time within the course of our cultural history. Both would also support the view that the presentation of the types of law has, on the one hand, a legal historical value as it points to the dependence of the historically changing of law on the changes in society and taking into account the changing of the individual while, on the other hand, it demonstrates that there exist certain laws and permanence with respect to human beings and society. The interpretation of such laws and their permanence through psychological typology emphasizes the projection of people's cognitive elements and the prevailing social or collective cognitive elements into the law of a specific time and place. Despite the fact that law changes together with the society *(Ubi societas ibi ius)*, it is still possible to establish certain specific, typical appearances of the law of a certain time. On the basis of such, there is the possibility to create certain specific types of law, the characteristics of which reflect the most typical or prevailing elements of the society in general at a certain time and place.

Weber and Jung would also agree that at a certain historical period the matter does not concern pure types of law but the co-existence of several types and their mutual presence to a certain extent in each other, concerning which one of them is prevalent or predominant and others being complementary to the prevailing one. Nevertheless there are differences between their comprehension of the types so Jung's more developed general theory of types will serve to criticize, change, reallocate or extend Weber's specific types of law in the context of legal historical development.

In the next paragraph, by referring to the characteristics of the psychological cognitive types presented above, I will be analyzing Weber's specific types of law through the individual periods of legal history and also trying to modify them.

3.3 General and Specific Types of Law

Weber's description of the specific types of law seems to still be applicable to a certain extent, which is also supported by their interpretation below made in light of Jungian psychological typology. However, a certain correction of his models or their understanding is necessary when the (post)Jungian psychological typology is applied to them.

Thus, Weber's specific types of law are to some extent modified so that the pages below consider the following general types of law: the religious type, the traditional type, the logical, and the harmonious type. The modification of Weber's thought through an analysis from the perspective of Jungian and post-Jungian psychological typology thus contributed to the development of a certain number of changes with respect to Weber's types of law: (i) certain types' names were altered; (ii) certain subtypes were allocated from one to another type of law; as well as (iii) certain new types of law and their subtypes were designed. On the basis of the application of the psychological typology Weber's four main types are to some extent renamed and additional four subtypes and their corresponding ideal persons or (legal) professionals are thereby developed.

Moreover, it is necessary to emphasize that within a particular period of time, along with a certain type of law, there also existed other types of law that were perhaps not so dominant in that era. Furthermore, until modern times it is not possible to consider any kind of established and consciously developed system of law – at least not in terms of the complexity which is typical of legal systems today.

3.3.1 The Religious Types of Law

The first general type of law described here is the so-called religious type of law. It consists of two variants: mystic law and theological law. To some extent, both types would correspond to what Weber called the charismatic revelation of law and theocratic law. Contrary to Weber, who in his ideal types referred to different epochs in which these two types appeared, I am analyzing the types within one general type of law that is not limited to one special period of time but can be present at any time and in any society. Mystic law and theological law are different from each other and they appeared in different time periods, with the first being applied in more primitive societies and the latter in more developed social systems. What then justifies them being analyzed within one joint model?

One of the main reasons for their unified treatment is the fact that both of them are based on intuition as one of the irrational cognitive functions. Still, they differ in that one is based on the auxiliary cognitive function of feeling whereas the other on the auxiliary function of thinking. This difference will be analyzed in more detail below with respect to a specific type.

3.3.1.1 Mystic Law

The first subtype of law refers to the activity of charismatic authority by prophets and mystics possessing supernatural capabilities. The people of that time generally believed in such interpreters of the interventions of divine forces, respected them as such and considered their authority to be legitimate. A type of law that is based on the operation of supernatural forces and their revelation to human beings is designated as the prophets' religious type of law. Such an irrational manner of referring to the divine origin of codes and other laws is particularly typical of the ancient Oriental law and its explicit theocratic orientation. To a certain extent, it also continued in ancient Greece, despite the important emergence of rationality, and at the early beginnings of Rome. Its importance, however, re-emerged during the Middle Ages, only to be subsequently slowly repressed with the beginnings of the modern era. What then followed was the increasing predominance of modern law being particularly secularized and rationalized. In the continuation we are presenting certain typical examples taken from legal history to demonstrate the existence of typical metaphysical elements in the perception of law.[4]

In view of law creation as a typical example of such religious law we can take the prologue to the Code of Hammurabi from almost two thousand B.C. In this work it is written that Hammurabi composed the mentioned code following a command from the God Marduk who had ordered him to ensure law and justice for his people (Korošec 53–55). A similar divine ordering was found even some 320 years before Hammurabi in the Law Collection of Ur-Nammu, where the God Nana ordered him to adopt certain legal rules (Rot 15–18). Also, the Decalogue revealed to Moses by God and which constitutes part of Hebrew law falls within this context. Furthermore, an important metaphysical element of the ancient Oriental law is reflected in trials by ordeal, divine judgements made upon the trial by, for example, a river,[5] duel, boiling water, fire, red-hot iron. In general, ordeals were carried out not only within the old Oriental law, but also in the Middle Ages, somewhat until the beginning of the thirteenth century when the Holy See prohibited priests from taking part in them (David, Grasmann 119).

Despite the increase of rationality in Ancient Greece, a certain degree of the metaphysical approach to law remained, especially at the beginning of Greek civilization. For example, Plutarch reported that King Lycurgus did not write down his laws as this was prohibited by one of the *retras*.[6] Furthermore, in his Great State Elegy, King Solon cited the divine laws of Dike (i.e. Lady Justice) (Sovre 76–79). Even in the strongly rationalized period of Rome, at least at its beginning during the period of the Kings of the archaic era prior to the Code of Twelve Tablets, one can find certain metaphysical elements when the Roman society lived upon customary law that still contained strong elements of sacral law. In such a manner they believed that a violation of law in the form of sacrilege or a crime interrupted the peaceful co-existence between people and gods. Also, the mentioned Code of Twelve Tablets still knew the punishment for desecration, which entailed that the perpetrator was given over to the gods and thereby became an outlaw (Škrubej 63). Subsequently, Roman law was rationalized to an important extent.

The irrational metaphysical elements in law were re-emphasized at the beginning of the Middle Ages when trial by ordeal was still used. Furthermore, a specialty of the early Middle Age law, particularly in Germanic *leges propria* (or *leges barbarorum*), were sworn assistants as persons who swore under oath that, for example, the assertion of one of both parties was correct or the defendant

[4] Examples are given according to the anthology by Škrubej (2010).

[5] A typical example of such follows from the Code of Hammurabi, in which one who accused another of, e.g., sorcery but could not prove such achieved that the accused was dipped in a river, and if the river threw him out so that he survived it was considered that he was innocent, so the one who had accused him was then executed (Korošec, *ibid*).

[6] This was an order by gods, which was communicated to people in the form of prophesy (Bratož 75).

was dangerous and thus probably guilty of committing a criminal offence. Otherwise the swearing under oath is a means of evidence that is in particular of sacral origin. In swearing under oath such assistants, not the witnesses in today's meaning, had to touch a sacred object, in the Christian era either the crucifix or gospel; in the case of Jews, the Decalogue. To some, a judgement sworn under oath was one of the first and the longest preserved forms of divine judgement (Vilfan 1996: 272).

At the time of the early Middle Ages, there still existed charismatic prophets who made judgements in specific procedures among the Germanic tribes in the West. Such prophets included, for example, the *brehon* in Ireland, *druid* among the Gauls, *rachimburgi* among the Franks and *lag saga* with respect to the Nordic tribes (Weber 768–769).

With this type of law, which is somewhat characteristic of the old Oriental law and also of the law of the early Middle Ages, there certainly co-existed other types of law that are presented in the continuation. In particular these referred to legal customs, their collections, the commands and decrees of various rulers, simple laws, court decisions, etc., which were not necessarily of a metaphysical origin. In addition to important sacral roots of the then societies it was also necessary to regulate completely secular issues. Thus, for example, even from old Mesopotamia, 2112 B.C., the notice on an 'ordinary' civil contract has been preserved (VerSteeg 2000).

Which are the most typical examples of the legal sources of general religious law?

If legally valid general legal acts with religious content are concerned, first of all the so-called metaphysical 'constitutions' must be mentioned, including the Bible (particularly the Old Testament) and the Koran. These were not only supreme religious documents but also applicable legal acts. Certain metaphysical legal norms also appeared in certain parts of historical laws or law collections such as the provisions of the Code of Hammurabi on ordeals. Certainly, until the appearance of modern legal codifications, all laws or codes were merely of a casuistic, not a systematic, character. Moreover, certain ritualistic legal customs that found their place in various law collections or were simply part of oral tradition could also have contained metaphysical laws. Otherwise the majority of laws in the past were in the oral form of legal custom until writing became better developed.

What occurred to such types of law in later periods? Thanks to the development of modern law, which is particularly rational, it was slowly pushed to a peripheral position. Already the shift in modern natural law transferred it from a sacral dimension to the dimension of an individual's moral perception of the world. With respect to the Anglo-American and European Continental legal families, today we could still find it but more or less in certain senses of justice or within a quite narrow circle of people who perceive law in relation to its classical (mostly religious) natural-law dimension. However, in the event of traditional and religious legal families it is still more common.

What, then, are the psychological-typological characteristics of prophets' and mystics' law? Which are their prevailing elements?

As we maintain that such law is irrational, one of the so-called irrational cognitive functions, as the functions of perception, must be in the forefront. Considering the fact that such a law depends to a large extent on divine revelation, the most important cognitive function in this respect is certainly introverted intuition. Concerning intuition (Lat. *intueri* to look upon, or in) Jung wrote that the content is presenting itself as a whole or entirely giving us little clue to discover or explain where it comes from. It concerns a somewhat instinctive perception of the given *(a priori)*, somewhat internal certainty or conviction. Spinoza and Bergson called the *scientia intuitiva* the highest kind of knowledge. According to Jung, both intuition and sensation are part of infantile and primitive psychology. In its introverted version, intuition also includes the visions and insights of various prophets and mystics who obtain the material for such in particular from the unconsciousness and archetypes (De Laszlo 1990).

Weber designated such an ancient type of law as irrational-formal. The 'formal' refers to the careful consideration of rituals which allegedly lead to one performing them to discovering a just judgment, while the 'irrational' certainly relates to the predominance of intuition as a special cognitive function. In such, the formality of a ritual or ritual procedures in discovering the contents of a just decision affords priests the possibility of shelter and security when they are dealing with powerful numinous contents.

Intuition as a perceptive function is irrational. To emphasize a perceptive function as dominant one entails that you consider an evaluative function to be of secondary importance. At least in the context of law and legal professions there is a difference between pre-modern law and modern law: as we will see in the continuation, the dominant cognitive functions in the framework of modern law are rational while in the pre-modern frame these were more irrational.

As already indicated, by adding an auxiliary function to the dominant function of intuition we initially come to the so-called mystic law. Here the auxiliary function, i.e. feeling, is an evaluative function as the one which evaluates the perception received through intuition. What feeling adds to intuition is a somewhat total, harmonic, and value-laden experience of numinous contents as revelation, which by the prophet is then shared with other people. In the context of legal procedures, it is the revelation that is relevant for the outcome of these procedures. Since we cannot deal with any type of legal professions at that time, we could at least point to a person typical of such law, that is a prophet or a mystic.

3.3.1.2 Theological Law

What I consider as the second type of religious law is the so-called theological law. It is intuitive in origin, being on one hand based on the perception of a metaphysical content but it is, on the other hand, different from mystic law. I call it theological law as, in terms of psychological typology, it can be considered that, after the period of mystical religious revelations from the period of the old Oriental law and the beginning of the Middle Ages, the theocratic authority of the Catholic Church in particular slowly became more dogmatic and thus departing from the so-called 'living' faith.

The religious contents once revealed were subsequently written down, codified and also dogmatized. A system of religious rules, procedures, and institutions was developed. This would entail that the initial, strongly intuitive, perception of the sacred was later evaluated by the auxiliary function of thinking, which is represented by logic, systemization, and formality. The aetiology of theology is Gr. *Theo* – God + –*logia* from *logos* – knowledge, study. Out of original religious revelation a comprehensive rational system of the religious teaching was developed. Notwithstanding the role of thinking in the development of the system of, e.g., canon law the primacy of intuitive perception must have been preserved since without a relation with the numinous content there is no religion, nor religious law.

This kind of orientation towards theological law is certainly represented by a typical person or profession, namely a theologian (or sometimes a priest). In the West, numerous theologians and canon lawyers have contributed to the development of a vast corpus of canon law. Likewise, in the Islamic Sunni tradition there have been various schools of law (like the Hanafi school of law), which were composed of theologians and lawyers and which contributed significantly to the subsequent development of Islamic law by interpreting various primary religious texts.

3.3.2 *The Traditional Types of Law*

Within the general traditional type of law I analyze two specific types of law that are typical of a traditional society: (1) imperial law and (2) customary law. As we will see in the continuation, both are characterized by the role of the predominant cognitive function of sensation, also as a function of perception being irrational in nature. In the first variant the dominant sensation is supported by the auxiliary (evaluative) function of thinking, while by feeling in the second variant.

This kind of law is traditional by its origin and as such more part of the pre-modern periods of time (i.e. partly in ancient times and the Middle Ages). Some traces of it can also be found today. Legal customs (e.g. constitutional customs in the UK, legal customs in business law) are not so uncommon today even in the most developed countries while imperial laws emerge from time to time in some absolutist political regimes (most frequently associated with some military commands during or after certain *coup d'etats*).

3.3.2.1 Imperial Law

In the sense of traditional law, Weber primarily dealt with the creation of imperial law (e.g. through commands by a ruler) regarding secular authority. *Imperium* signifies direction, command, or supreme power. Thereby Weber in general considered the power and commands of military commanders at the time of the Great Migration at the end of the Roman Empire. At that time, many wars and military conflicts occurred when the tribes had to act very quickly, most often merely upon an oral command, which could temporarily repeal and substitute even the traditional customary law of a certain tribe. Such imperial law was subsequently developed in the period of patrimonialisation (Lat. *patrimonium* from *pater* father), being a kind of privatization of public authority by local feudal lords at a micro level, and emperors in the event of the macro level of the kingdom. Such mostly oral laws, supplemented local legal customs and, through social development, led to more rational forms of legislation.

Such patrimonial law was not rational in the sense of logical rationality, since the ruler made his decisions case by case exercising discretion most often without being bound by any prior legal rules. So the result of a certain procedure was to a great extent dependent on the ruler's grace or privilege which he or she vested in someone. If the ruler was simultaneously the highest priest in the kingdom then his power was almost complete (Weber 844–845). Still his or her discretion was not absolute since he or she had to some extent consider also local customs and religious norms (of natural law).

The patrimonial authority of this kind was patriarchal (Gr. *patriaches* from *patria* generation) or "father-like". In the language of symbols, the father archetype represents the cognitive function of sensing, which primarily refers to "earth law" (Chetwynd 38).[7] The legal sources of such imperial law were various, mostly oral commands or directions in the sense of individual legal acts, for example in terms of the number of days that a serf had to spend at a castle performing compulsory work. Added to this could be various gifts of land or land tenures, usually made in writing as statements of will by which feudal lords donated land to their vassals as *alodium* or in return for military service. Furthermore, there are also Capitularies issued by Frankish kings and which contained instructions for the regulation of certain areas in royal ownership. These were, however, more similar to what we call today general legal acts although they were written in a more casuistic fashion.

As already mentioned rulers, emperors, chieftans, and other types of leaders have traditionally been considered as authorities of a father-like character for a particular social group. At the same time they had a role of supreme earthly authority. They had to resolve concrete and very much practical problems usually very fast since their tribe would be in serious jeopardy. There was no time for reflection or rational decision-making with the resulting calculation of pros and cons. Hence the sensing function in the forefront of such decision-making as natural-like reaction to a physical danger. In terms of perception, such authority is directed by concrete, practical, and real issues to be decided upon. Their authority stems from a traditional need for social order and social rules to be obeyed. The sensing cognitive function is supported by the auxiliary function of thinking (when time for reflection is available) such as when the ruler is not directly engaged in a

[7] Father is a symbol of reproduction, possession, ruling, and virtue (Chevalier, Gheerbrant 398).

combat. The sensing perception of reality is thus evaluated in a thinking manner: logically in terms of utilizing a certain means to cause a certain effect, impersonally regardless of the consequences for whichever person (in a cold-blooded fashion of an absolutist: "because I want it so since I am God's representative on the earth"), and in a tough way by means of standing firm on a decision reached by wishing it to be implemented quickly and efficiently.

A person typically responsible for such types of law is the ruler or the emperor (of a more absolutist type).

3.3.2.2 Customary Law

Traditional law is also reflected in numerous legal customs. In addition to metaphysical law these were very much typical of pre-modern law, all the way from the ancient Oriental law, ancient Greece, partially Rome, to the Middle Ages in the framework of which they even represented its 'constitution' due to their importance for the legal sources of that historical period. Legal customs had to be respected even by rulers not only in the old Oriental law but also throughout the Middle Ages (Grossi 29–30), the origins of legislation from the Middle Ages being collections of legal customs (either of the nobility, emerging cities, or agrarian communities) (Vilfan 1991: 84–85). They were, however, marginalized by the great legal codifications of civil law. For example, the Austrian Civil Code *(ABGB)* provided that customs did not legally apply by their mere existence "but only if a certain law explicitly referred to them" (Škrubej 267). In today's predominantly rational law, legal costumes very rarely count as formal legal sources.[8]

Legal is considered to be only that custom, i.e. a certain (incessant) repetition of an activity, which a community recognizes as mandatory and valid. As such, it seems to be connected with the cognitive function of sensing that gives much weight not only to the perception of certain facts but also to the norm or obligation existing therein, and particularly values positively what is unchangeable. Sensing as a perceptive function is irrational in character. With respect to legal custom, this is reflected in somewhat blind trust in traditional legal customs, in their repetition also merely for the sake of themselves, even if it is often not very rational and would be more reasonable for them to be altered (De Laszlo 1990). If a person with the predominant intuitive function trusts more in possibilities and is by his or her nature inclined to change, the sensory type is more bound by actuality, values conservativeness positively and respects customs and tradition. In short, such a person accepts the world and values as they are (Briggs Myers, Myers 57–58). One of the elements of the function of sensing is also tradition, respecting continuity, social affirmation, which is ensured by established institutions and already known

[8] They may apply as, e.g., commercial usages or legal standards in civil law. As formal legal sources they also appear in constitutional and international law. In the framework of modern law they tend to be codified.

methods. Concerning this, the sensing as a cognitive function is disinclined to changes and unconventional departures from established norms (Quenk 10).

Contrary to imperial law, the auxiliary function typical of customary law is feeling. (Legal) customs are social norms which grow organically in society. They are reflections of complex and interconnected relationships between people, values, morality, and interests. As such they are evaluated in the manner of a total experience as being overarching and comprehensive social norms that are valid since time immemorial, unlike today's legal norms which are of a known creator and limited duration. In their creation they are the products of an entire society and its need for social regulation. Furthermore, being based on concrete issues they are much closer to the personal needs of individuals than the abstract and general legal rules of modern legislation.

Typical persons for such a type of law would be elders[9] in a society as the guardians of its customs. This is further supported by the fact that in pre-modern societies it was older people particularly that were asked to describe the substance of (legal) customs for the purpose of demonstrating a valid law for the purpose of resolving a particular (legal) dispute.

Finally, from the view of legal history, we can find another flaw in Weber's theory of the ideal types of law. Here the problem is that, despite his very complex analysis of legal history within the traditional type of law, he does not even mention legal customs although these are considered by legal historians to be among the most important sources of law until the beginning of the creation of modern law.

3.3.3 *The Logical Types of Law*

Although in the framework of this type of law I analyze what Weber described as (a) legal honoratories' law and (b) systematic law, and which is sometimes depicted as rational law when Weberian ideal types of law are dealt with, I use a different name. I call such a type logical law. The reason for this is to differentiate it from another type of law which I call harmonious law, which is also a rational type of law. Both logical law and harmonious law are rational since the dominant cognitive functions behind both of them are rational: in the case of logical law thinking and in the event of harmonious law, feeling. Another argument for calling this type of law logical is also the fact that both subtypes or specific types of logical law are very much logical: which is characteristic of the casuistic type of law is induction and, for systematic law, deduction, both being logical methods.

To claim that logical law is only a product of the modern law or the modern state, and not at all of other historical periods, would be mistaken from the viewpoint of legal history. It is more than certain that parts of logical law existed in the past, even

[9] In some local communities such persons could also be mayors. In Frankish law *(Lex salica)* there was a *tunginus* as a person who performed the judicial function.

before the period of ancient Greece which is generally considered as marking the major break of *logos* with *mythos* (Kaufmann 51). Nevertheless, the old Oriental law, if its rationality could be maintained at all, was even in its rationality highly permeated with metaphysical and traditional law. Thus, in the Code of Hammurabi we can trace certain rational parts that are to some extent connected with metaphysical elements (e.g. in the case of ordeals) as well as with traditional elements (e.g. in the event of a certain custom that was incorporated in the Code). Moreover, one of the important differences between modern legal societies and pre-modern legal societies is in that the modern law is predominantly rational given the fact that metaphysical and traditional elements are quite rare in such laws. As already pointed out, contrary to the Western systems of Anglo-American law and the European Continental law, customary law as traditional law and metaphysical law have been preserved much more in the heterogeneous group of the traditional and religious legal systems of non-Western societies (e.g. in Africa, the far East and in Islamic countries).

In this section I differentiate between two subtypes of the general rational type of law. First, the logical-casuistic type of law is presented, and secondly the logical-systematic type of law is dealt with.

3.3.3.1 Casuistic Law

The logical-casuistic type of law is of an older origin than the logical systematic type, although it is still present in contemporary legal systems. Various statutes adopted already in the ancient Oriental law, ancient Greece and Rome, indeed all until the period of the great legal codifications, were mainly of a casuistic character, since they broadly referred to the factual situations in which legal norms were to apply. In no sense was there a systematization and regulation of substance in the manner it is known today and which was in particular typical of the legal codifications of the nineteenth century (e.g. *Code civil*, Austrian *ABGB*, German *BGB*). Roman law also belongs to this type of law as it was to a greater extent not codified until Justinian in the sixth century (in the *Corpus iuris civilis*). By its systematization the *Corpus* can hardly be compared with modern codifications, which signifies that that kind of rationality was not yet developed in the human psyche of that time. As already indicated, the logical-casuistic law is to an important extent also found in the contemporary Anglo-American legal family, especially concerning judicial common law, in which the judge has been historically the most important legal figure, although in recent times systemization has gained importance with the increase of legislation activities.

What is important for the logical-casuistic type of law in terms of psychological typology is the primacy of the cognitive function of thinking as the main function supported by the auxiliary function of sensation. For the thinking function, the operation of logic in the sense of relying on logical analysis, cause and effect, sequential justification, impartiality in decision-making, etc., are typical. The sensation function contributes to the red thread of thinking by directing it into concreteness, reality, practicality, experiment, and tradition (Quenk 10–11). Today this is among other areas of law also mostly typical of judicial practice or case law. In such a manner it is possible to comprehend Weber's rationality-substantive law as its thinking-sensing dimension. Thus, a legal profession typical of this type of law will certainly be a judge, but also an attorney (lawyer) would very easily fall within this specific type.

3.3.3.2 Systematic Law

The second previously mentioned subtype of logical law can be called the logical-systematic. This is typical of the subsequent development of law that culminated in modern legal codifications and is today mostly characteristic of general legal acts (such as constitutions and statutes, executive regulations, treaties). To Weber it signified the last step in the development of people's rationality. Here the main thinking function is supported by the auxiliary function of intuition, characteristic of which are: abstractness, conceptuality, and theory. Thus abstractness is in the psychological-typological sense focused on concepts and abstract meanings of ideas and their interrelations. Furthermore, conceptuality means focusing on mere concepts and not their application, it also entails complexity. Finally, the emphasizing of the theoretical is typical of searching for models and relations between abstract concepts (Quenk, *ibid.*). In this sense it is possible to understand Weber's rational-formal dimension of law – as the thinking and intuitive dimensions, the latter mostly in the sense of abstractness and conceptuality. Such an approach has traditionally been more typical of the European Continental legal family than of others, and which in the past professors contributed to its development, particularly in faculties of law.

The persons or (legal) professionals that would fall under this category are certainly modern legislators, the historical ideals of such being the great codifications of the nineteenth century. Furthermore, as mentioned above, we should add to this type of law also professors of law, in particular those from the European Continental legal family whose legal science, in the process of the reception of Roman law from the twelfth century onwards and in the development of *ius commune*, have contributed immensely to the codifications.

The legal sources that are typical of the logical-casuistic subtype of law are certainly judgments of courts as individual legal acts that have an *erga omnes* effect when being precedents. What are typical of this subtype were also the opinions of classical jurists in Rome, which during Augustus' Principate had been pronounced by the Emperor's authority. In ancient times legislation was also adopted, however, until the time of the modern codification movement such legislation was mostly of the casuistic type rather than systematic. The codifications from the beginning of the nineteenth century are mostly typical of the logical-systematic type of law, which today includes mostly constitutions, statutes, and executive regulations as general legal acts.

'Contemporary' law, particularly that of the logical character, either concerns the systematic or the casuistic type of law. This signifies that there is much less presence of the traditional and the metaphysical elements in law than it was the case in the past.

3.3.4 *The Harmonious Types of Law*

Quite a few legal theorists today write about certain new elements of law that are emerging in order to show that we need to deal with a special type of law that they call sometimes contemporary or postmodern law. Such a kind of new law complements modern law in the same manner that the classical characteristics of modern law (including generality, abstractness, systematization, logic, formality (Perenič 1981) under the umbrella of the so-called instrumental rationality (*ratio*),[10] are being complemented by other elements.

In this context what is recently not only popular, but also increasingly important, is alternative dispute resolution (ADR), which is represented by various procedures of negotiation, conciliation, mediation, arbitration, early neutral evaluation, building a consensus process, etc. Nevertheless ADR has its own history. Thus, as early as 1800 B.C., the Mari Kingdom (in modern Syria) used mediation and arbitration in disputes with other Kingdoms. Between 1200 and 900 B.C. the Phoenicians (in the eastern Mediterranean) practiced negotiations, while in 500 B.C. an arbitration system called *Panchayat* was used in India. Then in 400 B.C. the Greeks used a public arbitrator in city-states so that even 100 years later Aristotle praised arbitration over courts. Also, in China in 100 B.C. the Western Zhou Dynasty established the post of mediator. Also interesting are the research results of different anthropologists and sociologists studying the role of ADR in traditional societies (e.g. among the Bushmen of Kalahari, Hawaiian Islanders, the Kpelle of Central Liberia, and the Abkhazians of the Caucasus Mountains) (Barrett, Barrett 2–19).

Thus, such harmonious law has had a huge importance in the historical development of, e.g., Chinese law. According to the teachings of Confucianism and the concept of *'li'* there developed a variety of forms of conflict-resolution outside the courts which were performed by family heads, close or distant relatives or simply society elders (Zweigert, Kötz 291). The *li* means appropriate behavior and determines social rules for each situation differently, i.e. involving relations between superior and inferior, between older and younger, nobleman and citizen, between relatives, friends, strangers, father and son, older and younger brothers, or husband and wife. These rules of behaviour allegedly represent the natural order. "This reflects the Confucian doctrine which sees legislation as a necessary evil, only to be invoked where the state must impose a criminal sanction because the cosmic order has been very seriously disturbed, or where the organization of the state

[10] This kind of rationality was severely criticized by Horkheimer (1974).

administration is in issue." (Zweigert, Kötz 288–290) In China, this perspective was very important at least until the second part of the nineteenth century when it became more Western-oriented, taking its example for legal regulation from various European legal codes. Moreover, a similar situation existed in Japan, at least until the *Meiji* period at the end of the nineteenth century, where the traditional "natural-law" rules were called '*giri*' (David, Grasmann 440).

Furthermore, also in the Continental Europe of the Middle Ages, arbitration was for a certain period of time more important than adjudication. The role of arbitration was not so much in helping someone to exercise his or her right but to maintain peace within a society and calm the conflicting groups. In his First Letter to the Corinthians, Paul recommended love instead of justice and advised believers not to bring their claims to courts but rather submit them to priests and brothers. At that time they considered law as something bad due to its earthliness, being as such at a low level of moral importance (David, Grasmann 108).

These were only few landmarks from the past in the development of ADR. It seems that such harmonious laws have always been present around the globe, in some societies and periods of time more than in others. Still it appears that it has never been used to the extent to which it is used today. How this version of law differs from typical modern (logical) law follows in the continuation through the prism of psychological typology.

The thinking rational evaluative cognitive function is typical of the "classical" modern (or logical) law and it is based on logical analysis that is focused on objectivity and impartiality and is close to binary thinking (Novak 2011: 140–177). Pursuant to such, one wins and another loses a lawsuit, one is either guilty or is not guilty for a criminal offense, one is obliged or not to pay alimony since in such cases *tertium non datur* applies. However, ADR most often concerns a different type of evaluation or decision-making. What is more decisive for such is the cognitive function of feeling as an evaluative function that steps out of the framework of logical rationality and formality and corresponds much more to the qualities of sympathy, compassion, harmony, compromise, mutual adaptation etc. (Quenk 11).

I call such a type of law 'harmonious' since maintaining social harmony, both in terms of individual relations among the people and in the society as a whole, seems one of the most important elements of the feeling function. If the logical type of law resolves disputes in a society in a binary fashion that most often has detrimental effects for further social relations, as already mentioned one of the goals of the harmonious type of law is to keep social relations going on by not ruining them. Concerning the logical type of law, with its dominant function of thinking, there could be some reference, even a connection, to the general (cultural) principle of Logos as its peculiar qualities are "to discriminate, reason, judge, divide, and understand in a particular way". The 'Logos culture' "insists upon giving voice to an idea, designating it, giving a name, making a concept, expressing it". On the contrary, the feeling function can to some extent be linked with the general (cultural) concept of Eros, which is "a principle of relatedness, seeking things together, gathering things together, establishing relations between things [...] leave things *in suspenso*; they have not necessarily to be said." However, Jung warned that the concepts of Logos and Eros are intuitive concepts which entails that they cannot be fully defined, but only referred to some small extent (Jarret (ed.) 102–104). For this very reason they are neither synonymous with thinking and feeling, nor simply attributable to a general difference between men and women.

Concerning this, ADR, with its important emphasis on the feeling function, does not concern fighting binary (black or white) solutions, as in the case of a classical judicial manner of resolving disputes, but rather the peaceful pursuit of compromise solutions by which a dispute can be resolved. It is similar to a therapeutic process in which a mediator (therapist) mediates between two parties (clients or patients), but not in a cold-logical objective and impartial manner which is completely detached from the parties. Instead, he or she is more of a counsel – subjective and partial – but equally with respect to both parties so that he or she leads them together to a solution not apart from each other in the system of winner or losers. The results of such an ADR procedure are not black or white but grey areas, i.e. compromises. Nevertheless, such a kind of decision-making is still rational since feeling is a rational cognitive function of evaluation.

In the U.S., where such a kind of dispute resolution has been widespread in recent decades, ADR methods and approaches not only include the above mentioned types of dispute resolution but also preventive law, therapeutic jurisprudence, case resolving courts, methods of creative dispute resolution, building consensus procedures etc. (Daicoff 169–196). Lawyers who are engaged in such areas of dispute resolution emphasize the importance of human relations, values, goals, emotions, which is very much typical of the above mentioned cognitive function of feeling, or the so-called ethics of care or empathy (Daicoff, *ibid.*). These approaches emphasize in particular altruism, non-materialism, non-competiveness, and oppose adversary court battles which are typical of modern law. Instead of black-and-white outcomes of court "fights" that only resolve disputes with respect to past facts and conflicts, ADR deals with a holistic approach that also looks to the future.

Following the two-subtypes pattern from the rest of the above discussion with regards to the psychological-type impact on developing the specific ideal types of law, is it possible to develop two specific types of law within the general harmonious type? Perhaps we could make a distinction between those ADR procedures that are closer to classical legal proceedings and those that are more atypical. In the first group we could find arbitration as being closer to traditional or classical legal procedures. To some extent, arbitration follows traditional law-like ways of resolving disputes, does not depart so much from established legal institutions, procedures and norms, and from the past and present situations in which the parties who submitted their dispute to the arbitration are. Thus it seems that arbitration and arbitrators as persons or (legal) professionals typical of this kind of dispute resolution are closer to the sensing function, which in this case would be the auxiliary cognitive function supporting the dominant feeling. Contrary to that mediators as persons or professionals which are typical of mediation would fall within the second group of the ADR. Contrary to arbitration, mediation is more distant from classical and traditional legal procedures than arbitration. It is particularly mediation that tries to find the most creative possible solutions for dispute resolution in order to keep established relationships going. Good mediation should be imaginative and value possibilities over tangibles and should also be original by valuing uniqueness and inventiveness. All these facets are characteristic of intuition being the auxiliary cognitive function that is typical for mediation in support of the dominant feeling function.

Finally, on the basis of the above-presented general and specific types of law and the persons, (legal) professionals, and legal sources associated or even typical of them as well as the historical periods in which these types dominated, it seems that the following table may be created (Table 3.1).

In light of these different historical types of law that underline the already mentioned general principle that law as a distinct social phenomenon is society-grounded not only in terms of place but also time, it remains to see what that means for a theory which has general and universalist ambitions, such as the one being developed here.

Table 3.1 The general and specific types of law in history

General types of law	Specific types of law	Ideal persons/ professionals	Cognitive functions[a] Dominant	auxiliary	Typical legal sources
Religious law	Mystic law	Mystic, prophet	N	F	Revelations of law
	Theological law	Theologian, priest	N	T	"Codified" religious law (canon law, Sharia law)
Traditional law	Imperial law	Ruler, emperor	S	T	Commands, old statutes
	Customary law	Elders, seniors	S	F	Legal customs
Logical law	Casuistic law	Judges, attorneys (lawyers)	T	S	Case law, legal opinions
	Systematic law	Legislators, law professors	T	N	Codifications, modern statutes
Harmonious law	Arbitration law	Arbitrators	F	S	Arbitration decisions
	Mediation law	Mediators	F	N	Mediation agreements

[a]The abbreviations for the cognitive functions within the Jungian psychological typology are as follows: *T* thinking, *F* feeling, *S* sensation, *N* intuition

3.4 Individual, Cultural Type Preferences, and a Type Theory of Law

Jung developed his theory of psychological types as a universalist theory since in his famous book on the types he argued about the existence of the same types in different geographical areas and different historical periods. Nowadays we would call such a theory a global one.

It is certain that Jung respected collective psychology as much as the individual one although when it comes to psychological typology he was mostly concerned with the individual characteristics of a psyche. Nevertheless he termed "collective all psychic contents that belong not only to one individual but to many, i.e., to a society, a people, or to mankind in general. ... Among civilized peoples, too, certain collective ideas – God, justice, fatherland, etc.- are bound up with collective feelings. This collective quality adheres not only to particular psychic elements or contents but to whole functions. Thus the thinking functions as a whole can have a collective quality, when it possesses general validity and accords with the laws of logic. Similarly, the feeling function as a whole can be collective, when it is identical with the general feeling and accords with general expectations, the general moral consciousness, etc. In the same way, sensation and intuition are collective when they are at the same time characteristic of a large group of men...." (Jung 1971: 417–218).

It is generally acceptable that Jung's model of analytical psychology has emphasized a cultural dimension from the very beginning as it can account for both the individual and collective phenomena in the framework of one's psyche. Cultural means here social or collective. After all Jung suggested the idea of archetypes of the collective unconscious as structuring elements in the psyche. They form a symbolic universe in which we live and express our individual and collective being. It is "a theory which acknowledges and celebrates plurality, the individual and cultural diversity across peoples and history..." (Hauke in: Alister, Hauke 295).

Even though his type theory was developed as a psychoanalytic theory based on the analysis of an individual psyche we could quite easily understand it socially. Likewise Walker tried to connect Jung with sociological theory. His purpose was to "place Jung on the sociological map: to show that his psychology is sociologically coherent". For that reason he wanted to link Jung's timeless theory of the psyche with a cultural theory of the psyche (Walker 53).

Moreover, there are at least two reasons for emphasizing a social relevance of Jung's types: (1) individual type preferences established against the background of the universalist type theory point to "natural" differences within a society; and (2) these individual type preferences, at a certain time and in a certain society, in one way or another contribute to cultural preferences by virtue of forming different cultural models. Here lies the great importance of the type theory for law as a typical social phenomenon, and for a legal theory as a special account trying to understand and explain that phenomenon.

There are at least two areas that are relevant for a legal theory to explain particular laws or legal systems in terms of cultural[11] type preferences: (a) geographical or comparative types of law (see above Sect. 2.3) and (b) historical types of law as historical type preferences concerning law (see above Sect. 2.4).

In the continuation I develop a type theory of law as a universalist theory of law, which to a certain extent is based on Jung's universalist type theory. As such, in an abstract manner as an ideal theoretical model, it presents possibilities with respect to general features of law when interpreted through psychological types. When concretized in terms of place and time, it explains and describes law through cultural type preferences applicable to law both geographically and historically.

References

Alister, I., & Hauke, C. (1998). *Contemporary Jungian analysis: Post-Jungian perspectives from the society of analytical psychology*. London: Routledge.

Barret, J. T., & Barret, J. P. (2004). *A history of alternative dispute resolution: The story of a political, cultural, and social movement*. Hoboken: Wiley.

Bratož, Rajko. (2003). *Grška zgodovina* [Greek history]. Ljubljana: Zveza zgodovinskih društev.

Briggs Myers, I., & Myers, P. B. (1980, 1995). *Gifts differing*. Mountain View: Davis-Black Publishing.

Chetwynd, T. (1982). *Dictionary for dreamers*. London: Paladin Books.

Chevalier, J., & Gheerbrant, A. (2006). *Slovar simbolov* [The symbols dictionary]. Ljubljana: Mladinska knjiga.

Daicoff, S. S. (2004). *Lawyer, know thyself.* Washington, DC: American Psychological Association.

David, R., & Grasmann, G. (1988). *Einführung in Die Großen Rechtssysteme Der Gegenwart.*

De Laszlo, V. S. (Ed.). (1990). *The basic writings of C. G. Jung*. Princeton: Princeton University Press.

Grossi, P. (2010). *Pravna Evropa* [Legal Europe]. Ljubljana: Založba/*cf.

Horkheimer, M. (1974). *Eclipse of reason*. London/New York: Continuum International Publishing Company Ltd.

Jarret, J. L. (Ed.). (1998). *Jung's seminar on Nietzsche's Zarathustra*. Princeton: Princeton University Press.

Jung, C. G. (1971). *Psychological types*. London: Routledge.

Kaufmann, A. (1993). *Einführung in Rechtsphilosophie und Rechtstheorie der Gegenwart*. Heidelberg: Muller Jur. Verlag.

Kirby, L. K., Kendall, E., & Barge, N. J. (2007). *Type and culture*. Mountain View: CPP Inc.

Korošec, V. (1954). Slovenski prevod Hammurabijevega zakonika [The Slovene Translation of the Code of Hammurabi]. *Zbornik znanstvenih razprav Pravne fakultete 24:* 53–55.

Novak, M. (2011). Legal thinking: A psychological type perspective. *Dignitas, 49*(50), 140–177.

Perenič, A. (1981). *Relativna samostojnost prava* [Law's relative independence]. Ljubljana: DDU Univerzum.

Quenk, N. (2009). *Essentials of Myers-Briggs type indicator assessment*. Hoboken: Wiley.

[11] On the importance of Jung's psychological types of different cultural contexes see, e.g. Kirby et al. (2007).

Roach Anleu, S. (2000). *Law and social change*. London: SAGE Publications.
Rot, M. T. (1997). *Law collections from mesopotamia and Asia minor*. Atlanta: Scholars Press.
Škrubej, K. (2010). *Pravo v zgodovini, Odlomki virov s komentarji* [Law in history, excerpts with sources with commentary]. Ljubljana: GV Založba.
Sovre, A. (1964). *Starogrška lirika* [Ancient Greek lyric poetry]. Ljubljana: Državna založba Slovenije.
VerSteeg, R. (2000). *Early Mesopotamian law*. Carolina: AP.
Vilfan, S. (1991). *Uvod v pravno zgodovino* [Introduction to legal history]. Ljubljana: ČZ Uradni list Republike Slovenije.
Vilfan, S. (1996). *Pravna zgodovina Slovencev* [The legal history of the slovenes]. Ljubljana: Slovenska matica.
Walker, G. (2012). Sociological theory and Jungian psychology. *History of the Human Sciences, 25*(I), 69.
Weber, M. (1978). *Economy and society*. Berkeley: University of California Press.
Zweigert, K., & Kötz, H. (1998). *Introduction to comparative law*. Oxford: Clarendon.

Chapter 4
Psychological-Typological Reading of Integral Theories of Law

Abstract Here I elaborate further on what I outlined in Chap. 2, how the different cognitive types influence the existence of different views on what is the question of the nature of law, or legal ontology. It follows due to the legal theorists' different predominant cognitive functions that we deal with different legal ontologies such as positive law and natural law, as well as with more contemporary ones that incorporate inclusive and exclusive positivist and non-positivist outlooks of the essence of law. The main focus is here, however, on the psychological-typological understanding of inclusive legal theories and then in particular the three-dimensional theory of law. It is the cognitive functions of either intuition or sensation as perceptive functions that most often determine the choice of the application of legal principles or legal rules, which can be designated as the dual-perception thesis. On the basis of psychological typology, the processes of law creation and law application could also be analyzed. What follows is an explanation of the importance of intuition in legal decision-making.

Keywords Inclusive legal theories • Psychological typology • Legal principles and legal rules • Three-dimensional theory of law • Law creation and law application • Intuition in law

4.1 How Can Inclusive Legal Theory be Understood Typologically?

In Chap. 1 of this book I discussed how inclusive legal theory as an integral theory of law differs from exclusive theories of law. Now we need to see how such inclusive legal theory can be understood typologically concerning psychological typology. At the beginning I will try to demonstrate how inclusive positivist theory of law can be read in a psychological-typological manner. Then I will make a similar presentation for inclusive non-positivist theory of law.

The 'positivistic' dimension of inclusive legal positivism emphasizes, first, the formal elements of a legal system. Here legal thinking is primarily oriented to the external (i.e. sensational or empirical) world of legal rules and facts or their interconnection. What comes into play in this aspect is the thinking apparatus as logical thinking that tries to find meaningful and necessary connections between

M. Novak, *The Type Theory of Law*, SpringerBriefs in Law,
DOI 10.1007/978-3-319-30643-8_4

facts and norms and between norms themselves. Such a process of evaluation, on the basis of empirical (or sensory) perception, can also be called empirical thinking or technical or instrumental rationality. In such a context, in the event of a clear or 'routine' case, the lawyer would operate as a 'technician' who carries out a simple logical operation of a deductive syllogism, as the legal premises for their decision-making are more or less clear. No doubt such clear cases can become unclear under certain circumstances, but this cannot overcome the idea, which one who is aware of what goes on in legal practice easily agrees with, that in the legal world there truly are a great number of clear cases. Such cases usually do not require much creativity to find proper major premises.

In the sense of its (instrumental) rational dimension, the 'positivistic' dimension of inclusive legal positivism also relates to its autonomy, a relative independent system of operation, a self-reflexive whole in the framework of legal certainty as the leading principle of such an empirical-thinking context. Such relation is justified by the concept of logical compulsion, in which, by virtue of interpretation or argumentation, lawyers try to justify the narrow legal character of a decision and present such as (logically) necessary. What is characteristic of the rationality which is supported by the mere empirical (sensual) world of facts and applying legal rules is concern for certainty, categorical self-sufficiency, and formal limits.

Second, the 'inclusivist' element of inclusive legal positivism suggests that in such an empirical-thinking context there is also a certain amount of room for intuition (of law or legal rules – Germ. *Rechtsgefühl*), which is in the service of (more rapidly) finding appropriate (empirically expressed) legal norms as such, under which the relevant facts will be subsumed. Such intuition is in the service of the previously mentioned instrumental rationality, so it could be named 'instrumental' (or extraverted) intuition.[1] It is not intended to create a new legal norm or essentially supplement such, so that it could be close to a new creation. It only serves the purpose of quickly and easily finding the relevant norm. Its value can certainly be tested through the process of evaluation and justification of the legal decision. Such instrumental intuition is more typical of inclusive legal positivist orientations, according to which the empirical (or sensual) prevails over the intuitive. This is even the case in the so-called hard or unclear cases in which judges may legislate, meaning that they may adopt a certain rule that is appropriate for the resolution of a problem. Even here intuition can play an important but not decisive role for the resolution of a case.

A lawyer who decides a case may also have certain moral intuitions, as everyone has them, but, according to inclusive legal positivists, within a context of legal norms and legal procedures these should not be decisive for deciding the case. But to some extent, extraverted or instrumental intuition is typical of exclusive legal positivists as well. They would also recognize some sort of legal 'sense' when trying to find legal norms applicable to a certain set of facts. Perhaps a difference in

[1] I have previously named it 'extraverted' intuition in order to contrast it with internal or 'creative' intuition, which would refer to internal or moral principles (e.g. of natural law).

this respect between exclusive legal positivists and inclusive legal positivists would be that the latter, unlike the former, would recognize the role of certain moral intuitions in the process of the establishment of the most fundamental norms in a given society that are important for co-existence and hence the survival of the same. However, irrespective of moral intuitions, what are important for inclusive legal positivists are mostly the empirical legal rules that constitute a legal system. And if such no longer correspond to people's moral intuitions, they should be changed following a specific legal procedure. Once again, for inclusive legal positivists what are decisive are valid legal rules which might be of a certain moral character, which, however, is not decisive for their legal validity. For example, justice, morality, and human rights are relevant only in so far as they are part of the context of valid legal norms. In a sense, their legal form, which makes them legally valid, is more important than their legal substance, their legality more important than their legitimacy.

Hart, as already shortly indicated at the beginning of this book, was certainly on the side of inclusive legal positivism, which presupposes that there is some connection with law and morality but that such is not essential for the concept of law. In his concept of law Hart included a minimum level of morality, which was, however, subordinate to and not very important for existing legal rules (the so-called 'minimum content thesis'). According to Hart, there are a number of natural features ("natural truisms") existing in society which to some extent determine the content of law as it must exist if it is to be viable as an institution consistent with the minimum purpose of human survival. Such natural truisms include, for example, human vulnerability, limited resources, and the fact that people are "neither angels nor devils". They point to the conclusion that laws must have a bare minimum of moral content if they are to serve their functions as law. Thus, Hart opposed the exclusive legal positivist perception that law may have any content since, in his opinion, the content of law is constrained by a natural connection between law and basic natural needs, but he also decisively rejected the conceptual connection between law and morality or justice (Hart 193–200). Furthermore, among the inclusive legal positivist there is also Coleman, who claims that morality is not necessarily excluded nor necessarily included in the concept of law, but is incidental to the concept of law (Coleman 316).

However, in the case of inclusive non-positivists, it seems that intuition plays a more important role than for inclusive legal positivists, with their more emphasized sensory or empirical function – especially when it comes to unclear cases. Here, through intuition a component of value enters legal decision-making. Such intuition, which can be called 'creative' intuition, as it crucially participates in the creation of a new legal norm, or substantially supplements such because of its vague character, is often applied in the event of gaps in the law or when a bad law is criticized and subsequently altered. Most often in such cases new legal norms are 'created' on the basis of internally perceived moral norms. In the case of gaps in the law, being types of unclear cases, inclusive legal non-positivists try to apply such principles. When there is a bad or grossly unjust law a conflict occurs between the empirical-sensory cognitive function (reflected in positive legal norms) and the intuitive cognitive function (reflected in intuitive moral norms), which tends to be resolved in favor of the latter. We could call such type of thinking intuitive thinking, which is quite typical of inclusive non-positivist perspectives.

As already mentioned Radbruch was in the inclusive non-positivist's group of scholars. He argued that existing legal rules can be invalid only in extreme circumstances or exceptional circumstances, not as a general rule (Radbruch 1946). Moreover, for Dworkin the matter concerns the integration of legal rules and moral legal principles that play the decisive role in hard cases (Dworkin 1997: 4). To the inclusive non-positivist group we must certainly add Alexy's inclusive non-positivism, which deals with three dimensions that are connected and intertwining: authoritativeness, social efficacy, and material correctness (Alexy 13). Some understand such approach to the concept of law as interpretivism, in which the law of a certain state is not only the expression of social facts (either social conventions or political practices) to which legal positivists and legal realists refer, neither is it the expression of pure moral perspectives, which natural lawyers would argue. Law is crucially connected with interpretation, which as such is also based on values such that it necessarily includes moral elements since both legal interpretation and legal argumentation deal with a set of facts and values (Bertea 2009). Among interpretivists, in addition to Alexy, we must also particularly note Dworkin. Especially known is his idea that law is an interpretative concept, or an argumentative social practice, which cannot be exhausted by any catalogue of rules or principles (Dworkin 1986: 413).

When it comes to his concept of non-positivism, Alexy describes such as being the fact that law is a system of norms which (1) require correctness, (2) are composed of provisions of the constitution, which is socially effective, and these norms as such are not extremely unfair, as well as of norms that are adopted in conformity with such constitutions, as norms that express the apparent minimum of social effectiveness and which as such are not extremely unjust; and, finally, (3) also embrace the principles and other normative arguments on which the process or procedure of the application of law is based or should be based so that it can claim correctness (Alexy 2002: 127). According to him, law is an activity of value with social existence, so what is typical of the character of law is that it is a claim for both authority (also coercion) and correctness (Alexy 2008: 292–294).

In today's world of legal theory there is a whole array of inclusive legal theories. These try to harmonize or adjust empirical (descriptive, social) and intuitive (normative, moral) elements from the classic (exclusivist) legal theories. In one way or another, such theories try to integrate the normative and descriptive elements of law into a uniform concept of law. In that, the descriptive (factual or also empirical) element in law pertains more to a legal positivist orientation, while the normative (intuitive, moral) element pertains more to a non-positivist orientation towards the concept of law. Below we will see examples of how both exclusive and inclusive legal theorists would approach resolving an unclear case in the manner of applying legal rules or legal principles. What is presented below is also an interpretation of the significance of both legal rules and legal principles in terms of psychological typology.

4.1.1 Legal Principles and Legal Rules

Traditionally, an important difference between exclusive legal positivism and natural law as a typical version of exclusive legal non-positivism has been the different consideration of legal rules and legal principles. While natural law traditions have generally grounded their precepts on (metaphysical or moral) legal principles, as legal standards exclusive legal positivists preferred legal rules to legal principles, since for them the former are more reliable by being more precise and determinate than legal principles, which are abstract and vague. For example, it was particularly the abstract character of natural-law oriented principles, and thereby the connected vagueness of such that were major legal premises in the traditional common law courts of pre-nineteenth century England, which Bentham attacked in the legal positivist movement of his time (Zweigert, Kötz 260; MacCormick, Summers 482). Out of this positivist movement came the requirement that concerning future precedents not the "spirit" of a case before the court should be binding on future courts but the *rationes decidendi* of such a case,[2] which are generally narrower in scope than the principle (or "spirit") in such a case in that they more resemble legal rules than legal principles.

However, if the abstract character of legal principles has been disvalued by legal positivists, such at the same time has been an advantage for natural lawyers as, in their opinion, it is closer to the (super)natural dimensions to which human beings relate in one way or another, such as Nature, God, Reason, morality, etc.

Why is the difference or even conflict between legal principles and legal rules interesting from a typological perspective? Does such a difference bear some typological relevance? Behind such traditional distinction, which is also reflected in the dichotomy between the role of legal rules and legal principles, is there some rationale?

From the psychological study of Jung's four main cognitive functions it was established that it is characteristic of the intuitive cognitive function to prefer abstraction to concretization, the latter being more characteristic of the sensory cognitive function. From this aspect, sensing focuses mainly on what can be perceived by the five senses, while intuition, the 'sixth sense', focuses mainly on perceiving patterns and interrelationships (Briggs, Myers 1980).

From the above-mentioned study made by Quenk concerning the sensing-intuition difference, it seems that behind the legal rule-principle controversy there is also some typological grounding. Moreover, if we go back to the major epistemological dilemma between the rationalists and the empiricists, it is not difficult to infer from that that the rationalists (with their preference for 'intuitive thinking') more prefer the abstract character of legal principles than the empiricists (with their preference for sensory or 'empirical thinking'), who more prefer the concreteness of legal rules when compared with legal principles. Hence, the traditional misunderstanding between exclusivist natural lawyers and exclusivist legal positivists

[2] Or the 'letter' of a case.

concerning the issue of the relevance of legal principles and legal rules in the operation of law. According to this traditional dispute, the rationalists – usually more natural-law oriented scholars – more prefer to base their perception of the nature of law on legal principles, or at least include them as very important in their scheme of law, as some sort of inborn or *a priori* moral elements in human minds from which legal rules can only be deduced. In contradistinction to that, the empiricists, i.e. more legal positivist-oriented scholars, more prefer legal rules to legal principles, as the former are more concrete and determinate, being the result of peoples' agreements and conventions since, in their view, there are no *a priori* 'truths' about law, which can only exist *a posteriori* based on facts and norms as products of people's social activities.

In a specific case, let's say in the event of a gap in the law, how would different legal scholars from either a legal positivist or legal non-positivist circle approach such a problem associated with the principle-rule difference? In such a case they would be expected to answer the question of whether there exists a gap in the law and how they would fill it. In this respect, let us take the case of *Riggs v. Palmer* (New York, 1889),[3] which became famous particularly due to Dworkin mentioning it in his Taking Rights Seriously (Dworkin 1997: 23). In that case a New York court had to decide whether an heir named in the will of his grandfather could inherit under that will, although he had murdered his grandfather to do so. The court reasoned as follows: "It is quite true that statutes regulating the making, proof and effect of wills, and the devolution of property, if literally construed, and if their force and effect can in no way and under no circumstances be controlled or modified, give this property to the murderer." (115 N.Y. 506, 22 N.E. 189)

How would, for example, classical or exclusive natural lawyers resolve the above-mentioned case with respect to the dichotomy between legal rules and legal principles?

In such a case, exclusive natural lawyers would probably maintain that there was no true gap in the law as the judges should apply to the case at issue the indemonstrable principle of justice as a moral principle. Their inspiration for such position could certainly be Thomas Aquinas, who began his legal pyramid by taking into account indemonstrable moral principles or the first principles of natural law (*Lex naturalis*), which were allegedly engraved in the soul of human beings by God (*Lex aeterna*). Thus, in his theory of law principles played the most important part, which was not the case regarding positive legal rules (*Lex humana*), as in his opinion these were obviously subordinated to the legal principles of natural law. The purpose of human legal rules was only to punish those who violated moral legal

[3] Elmer Palmer was a 16-year-old who successfully prevented his grandfather from changing his will, of which he himself was the main beneficiary, by murdering him. After serving a prison sentence, there appeared to be no legal obstacle to prevent Palmer from claiming his inheritance. This was challenged in court by relatives who were minor beneficiaries, but the judge upheld his claims because the black letter of the law in relation to the will had been satisfied. This decision was overturned by a majority decision of the Court of Appeal, depriving Palmer of his inheritance, on the basis that no one should profit from their own wrongdoing (Tebbit 2000: 59).

principles and prevented them from doing that (Aquinas, I-II, q. 91, a. 1, a. 2, a. 3, c.; I-II, q. 95, a. 1; Clark 2000).

According to this version of exclusive natural law, the mentioned principle of justice is engraved in a human being's soul by God (*Lex aeterna*), thus becoming part of *Lex naturalis*. The way the (appellate) court reacted in *Riggs. v. Palmer* was a normal moral reaction to the evil committed by the testator's grandson. Also, according to such position of exclusive natural law, there was no need for such a principle to be written in a specific code as it can be intuitively perceived at any moment by the judge as a moral and reasonable person, by his moral conscience and intellect applied to a specific case.

A similar position to that of Aquinas, with respect to the mentioned problem of the murderer inheriting from the deceased so murdered, would also probably be taken by Finnis, as an exclusive non-positivist. According to Finnis, the act committed by the heir is certainly against the indemonstrable, self-evident, or absolute values or principles of natural law (Finnis 1981). Thus, he would probably continue that there was no gap in the law since one of the mentioned self-evident principles or values was applicable in that situation so the judges were completely right to have applied it. The principle of not profiting from one's wrongdoing that was applied by the judges (of the court of appeal) in that case surely meets the requirements of the principle of justice, if not also of other principles of practical reasonableness. Moreover, such deed committed by the heir was contrary to the "right not to have one's life taken directly as a means to any further end" as an absolute human right (Finnis 225).

Kelsen was on the other side of the exclusivists' spectrum, as a proponent of exclusive legal positivism. Kelsen based his Pure Theory of Law on legal norms as legal rules, in the framework of which there was no place for legal principles, let alone moral legal principles (Kelsen 1945, 1960). In relation to the above-cited case of *Riggs v. Palmer*, it seems that Kelsen also would not have approved the existence of a gap in the law, but for completely different reasons than Finnis. His well-known position concerning the existence of gaps in the law was negative. He opined that the legal order does not contain any gaps. When a judge deals with a law it is always possible to apply such a law. For this reason it is logically unacceptable to maintain that a legal order does not contain solutions. To allow a judge to find and fill a gap in the law would present an ideological or political blueprint for such to add legislative rules, which is not at all the task of judges (Kelsen 1945: 146–149, 1960: 251–255).

In the above mentioned case, a typical argument of his would be that finding a gap in the law would entail that judges could take advantage of it as a pretense for their judicial law-making, thus supplementing or amending statutes. In the mentioned case, if there was no specific legal rule in the provisions of the law on inheritance, the grandson would receive the property. However, if he was thus entitled to receive the testator's property following the mentioned law, the same property would perhaps be seized from him under, for example, criminal law provisions providing legal grounds for the seizure of objects obtained through criminal acts. Kelsen would also not tolerate immoral acts as such, but, instead of simply translating the same into legal reasons, he would rather find other "proper" legal reasons to prevent a person from benefiting from his wrongdoing. However, in *Riggs v. Palmer* Judge Gray dissented from the majority opinion rejecting the appeal, in Palmer's favor, by arguing that "the matter does not lie within the domain of conscience" since judges are "bound by the rigid rules of law, which have been established by the legislature" (Adams 1992: 138).

What about the inclusive legal positivist/non-positivist dilemma concerning the relation between legal rules and legal principles, from a typological perspective?

Inclusive (or 'soft') legal positivists include morality as a part of law, yet in their view its connection with law is only incidental and not essential for an understanding of the concept of law. In an unclear case they would surely not give precedence to a (moral) legal principle over a legal rule as their approach is more empirical than intuitive. For example, Hart primarily focused on legal rules rather than legal principles. In his major work, however, he to some extent accepted the (moral) principle of justice with the following words: "... because a minimum of justice is necessarily realized whenever human behavior is controlled by general rules publicly announced and judicially applied" (Hart 206–07). After this initial position regarding the minimum of natural law that to a minimum extent embraced at least the (moral) legal principle of justice, he primarily continued to deal with legal rules. This entails that legal principles in such legal theories are not of major importance, although to some extent they are recognized as legal standards.

How a majority of inclusive legal positivists considers the relation between legal principles and legal rules also follows from their opinion regarding how hard or unclear legal cases are (to be) resolved. Following Hart, in such a case the judge "must exercise his discretion and make law for the case instead of merely applying already pre-existing settled law. So in such legally unprovided-for or unregulated cases the judge both makes new law and applies the established law which both confers and constrains his law-making power [...] However, his powers are interstitial as well as subject to many substantive constraints." (Hart 272–73). Such constraints that prevent him from judging arbitrarily include reasons, values, principles, or other legal standards (Hart 273). "This is the importance characteristically attached by courts when deciding unregulated cases by analogy so as to ensure that the new law they make, though it is new law, is in accordance with principles or underpinning reasons recognized as already having a footing in the existing law" (Hart 274).

Accordingly, how then would Hart resolve the above-mentioned case of *Riggs. v. Palmer*? Hart would probably admit that in this case there was a gap in the law which failed to prohibit the murderer from inheriting the property of the deceased so murdered. In this manner, Hart would probably advise the judges to fill such a gap in the law by making a new legal provision regulating such, however, by resorting to some analogy with a similar provision (e.g. regarding intestate succession in the same statute, or prohibiting a wrongdoer from benefiting from his wrongdoing as determined in some other statute).

What about inclusive legal non-positivists? What would their position concerning these issues be?

If exclusive natural lawyers – or non-positivists, if we take a broader view of such – are extreme rationalists, then inclusive legal non-positivists are more moderate rationalists on the issue of the difference between the relevance of legal principles and legal rules, considering that they hold the empirical (sensory) part of law (such as legal rules) to also be very important (e.g. Dworkin, Alexy). Still, they consider (moral) legal principles even more important – especially when hard or unclear cases are to be resolved. In the view of the inclusive legal non-positivists, there is no *a priori* subordination of legal rules to legal principles or vice versa, as in the case of exclusive legal theories. According to them, the legal system is an integrity of legal rules and legal principles, following which the relation between these two legal standards has to be resolved on a case by case basis within the legal system. This was evident already from Radbruch, who insisted on the validity of legal rules, on the basis of the application of the legal certainty principle, as long as they do not grossly or extremely violate the principle of justice (Radbruch 1946).

Ronald Dworkin has re-introduced legal principles, which have not only legal but also moral importance, to the discourse in contemporary legal theory. It is well known that Dworkin's position was contrary to Hart's in that Dworkin's (ideal) judge would apply moral principles in hard cases since, according to him, judges are under a legal obligation which is imposed on them not by hard and fast rules but by a "constellation of principles" as well as rules (Dworkin 1997: 44), hence his position that there should be no gaps in the law since the judge can always apply a legal principle to any potential legal problem in the law (Dworkin 1986: 229).

In the above-indicated manner Dworkin's solution to *Riggs. v. Palmer* would be the same as the one reached by the judges in that case. If in that case statutes would allow the property of the deceased to be given to the murderer, Dworkin's position would match the reasoning of the court in that case, in the words of Judge Earl (Adams 137): "... all laws as well as all contracts may be controlled in their operation and effect by general, fundamental maxims of the common law. No one shall be permitted to profit by his own fraud, or to take the advantage of this own wrong, or to found any claim upon his own iniquity, or to acquire property by his own crime." (Dworkin 1997: 23). So the murderer would not inherit from the deceased so murdered.

Furthermore, the above-indicated conflict between the empiricists and rationalists, between those who in hard cases prefer legal rules and those who in such cases prefer legal principles, between sensory or "empirical" thinkers and intuitive thinkers, could also be applied to a recent disagreement between two important contemporary legal philosophers. Here I am referring to the disagreement between two different theoretical approaches concerning the balancing of principles (or fundamental rights) between Alexy and Habermas (Alexy 2005). This, in my opinion, interestingly reflects two different epistemological understandings of the same problem. In short, on one hand Habermas accused the legal method of balancing as being mere intuitivism, and as such even irrational, which diverts the focus of channels of legal deciding from the area that is determined by the concepts of right and wrong, correct and incorrect, to the area of more or less appropriate and discretion. On the other hand, Alexy opposed such position by arguing that balancing is still a rational activity that is supported by the rational structure of arguments.

In my opinion, their disagreement was not about the evaluation of such decisions as both would certainly support the idea that a legal decision must be reasoned by rational arguments that are as diversified as possible. After all, it is rational argumentation in the form of evaluation that makes modern law verifiable. Their disagreement was, in my view, more due to their different perception of rationality or, predominantly, thinking in terms of psychological types. On the one hand, in his concept of balancing Alexy allowed himself the rational-intuitive consideration of various degrees or nuances between principles (or fundamental rights) when they collide with each other. On the other hand, Habermas opposed such as being intuitive on the basis that in balancing, according to Habermas' conception of rationality, which is closer to empirical rationality than Alexy's, there are no previous concrete and tangible legal standards as in the case of legal rules pursuant to which such legal decision-making as balancing would be carried out. For that reason every balancing is allegedly arbitrary.

Finally, from the above-mentioned it seems that the Alexy-Habermas dispute in relation to balancing was not between irrationality and rationality, but between two types of rationalities, on the one hand intuitive rationality, and on the other hand empirical rationality. In the above-mentioned dispute concerning balancing, it seems that Alexy was closer to the rationalists' perspective on the issue of legal deciding, whereas Habermas was closer to the empiricists' viewpoint concerning legal deciding.

The above-mentioned leads us to what can be named the dual-perception thesis, which is an indispensable part of what I call the type theory of law as an integral theory of law, which among other things describes why is it possible that there occur such incompatible situations as exclusivist legal positions that try to be mitigated by virtue of inclusive approaches to the nature of law.

4.1.2 The Dual-Perception Thesis

In the context of a typological reading of legal theories, the cognitive function that decides whether we are dealing with one or another version of legal theory, be it exclusive legal positivism or exclusive legal non-positivism, is either intuition or sensation. In terms of Jungian psychological typology, both of them are so-called perceptive cognitive functions, and both of them are irrational since, unlike evaluation and thinking, which are rational, perception is irrational. Thus, as regards exclusive legal non-positivism (or natural law), it is intuition which is the decisive perceptive cognitive function, whereas in the case of exclusive legal positivism, sensation is more important. The predominant evaluative function concerning law is certainly thinking, as a rational cognitive function. As such, it has the role of evaluating what has been perceived either through sensation or intuition. To an important extent, thinking is determined by perception, either intuitive or sensory.

Thus, in the case of exclusive legal non-positivism (or natural law), we are dealing with 'intuitive rationality' as the type of rationality that is to an important extent determined by intuition. Such rationality can also be called 'intellect' or *Vernunft* (Germ.). In a similar manner, when exclusive legal positivism is concerned, there is an important, even determinative, influence of sensation on thinking. Such entails sensory or 'empirical' rationality, which is sometimes also called instrumental (Horkheimer 1974) rationality or simply *ratio*.

Frankly, it is much easier to establish interrelations between perceptive and evaluative cognitive functions with regard to extreme or exclusive legal theories than with regard to more moderate or inclusive legal theories. However, it is still possible to maintain that with respect to the mentioned two versions of inclusive legal theories, i.e. inclusive legal positivism and inclusive legal non-positivism, the influence of perceptive functions on thinking is not so great or extreme as in the case of exclusive legal theories. Nevertheless, in inclusive legal positivism sensation prevails over intuition when influencing thinking, whereas in inclusive legal non-positivism the situation is vice versa.

The distinction between legal rules and legal principles is to an important extent influenced by the above-mentioned dual-perception thesis. The difference between the two in this context is more than evident in the event of a hard case, e.g. a gap in the law. Consequently, let me conclude this chapter by summarizing the above-expressed positions of certain prevailing legal theories with respect to the distinction between legal rules and legal principles when applied to resolving such a hard case.

First, exclusive legal positivists, or natural lawyers (at least, e.g., Aquinas and Finnis), ascribe legal principles, especially those of moral content, prime importance in the legal system. If legal rules contradict such legal principles, which are even 'indemonstrable', they must be neglected or abrogated. Furthermore, there cannot be gaps in the law as there is always a legal principle, in one or another way directed by the common good, that governs any problematic situation. We have mentioned before that principles are by their character more abstract than rules, thus from a psychological-typological view, they are very much associated with the cognitive function of intuition, and rules, as more concrete than principles, with sensation. In such a case, the abstract element of a principle, and simultaneously the intuitive element, has a gross advantage in comparison with the concrete character of a rule, and therefore the sensory (or empirical) element.

On the other side of the spectrum of legal theories we find exclusive legal positivism. At least in Kelsen the situation is quite the opposite if compared with that of exclusive legal non-positivism. According to the first-mentioned school of legal thought, legal principles and thereby the abstract and intuitive elements do not play an important role in legal systems. There is a much greater emphasis on legal rules, and thus the concrete and empirical elements. They do not recognize the existence of gaps in the law, as there is always a legal rule (not legal principle) that resolves a potentially problematic legal situation.

What about 'inclusive' legal theories and the relation between legal principles and legal rules?

Inclusive legal positivism, at least in a Dworkinian version, places quite broad importance on legal principles whose existence is the reason why we cannot deal with gaps in the law. If a legal rule, which is characteristic of the concrete and sensory, comes up short, there is always a legal principle, thus the abstract and intuitive, to resolve the case at issue. However, the ratio between legal principles and legal rules is not so much to the advantage of the former as in the case of exclusive legal non-positivism. Unlike the position of exclusive legal non-positivism, according to inclusive legal non-positivism, legal principles are not indemonstrable in themselves, but part of a legal system or legal tradition that restricts their free application to some extent by imposing concrete and empirical restraints.

In the case of inclusive legal positivism, e.g. of a Hartian type, legal principles, as elements of the abstract and intuitive elements, are much less important than (concrete and empirical) legal rules. When a legal rule comes up short, there is no legal principle that governs the problematic legal situation, so a gap in the law occurs. In such a case, it is up to the judge and his or her discretion to adopt a supplementary legal rule. However, the concrete and empirical elements are to some extent subject to the minimum content of moral (or natural) law, which being abstract and intuitive is the starting point within nature for human beings to survive in society.

When it comes to taking a position about whether to support exclusive or inclusive theories of law I hope that I have already been clear enough with my type theory of law: I hope it will be a plausible argument in defending inclusivism in law and legal theory. Even though my type theory of law tends to be a descriptive one, as we will also see in the continuation, it seems to be able to normatively defend inclusivism. However, when it comes to a decision between inclusive positivism or inclusive non-positivism, we will see that as a predominantly descriptive theory law it unfortunately has no far-reaching answer. We will see that when the legal matter concerns an extreme (non-democratic or totalitarian) political situation it could well be a Radbruchian or inclusive non-positivist. Whereas in a "normal" (democratic) political situation I admit a certain role that hermeneutics has in the general framework of inclusive positivism.

Therefore, does it make any sense to say normative elements within a descriptive theory of law or non-positivist elements in the general frame of inclusive positivist theory of law? Before giving a final answer we need to see how the three dimensional theory of law can be interpreted in a psychological-type manner.

4.2 A Psychological-Typological Understanding of the Three-Dimensional Theory of Law

At the outset I mentioned that inclusive legal theory forms part of integral theories of law. Furthermore, as a special version of integral theory of law, I presented the three-dimensional theory of law. As I have already discussed the fundamentals of

Jung's type theory, it seems reasonable to see now how this three-dimensional theory can be comprehended in view of the psychological type theory.

Thus below I analyze the above-described three dimensions of law (i.e. legal values, legal relations, and legal norms) through the prism of an individual, more precisely through the prism of his or her basic cognitive functions. If we try to comprehend reality, of which law is just one part, psychologically we take into account the idea of projection or conception that external activities or results of peoples' actions to an important extent are reflections of their internal state of mind or their psychological predispositions.

In order to know what law is and how it appears we should examine certain psychological processes in an individual who takes part in creating and applying legal rules. Which psychological processes are carried out in lawyers as well as in laypersons when they play "legal games"? Such psychological processes can be observed both in the individual as well as collectively. What I am interested in here is mostly the perspective of an individual person, his or her trying to understand and participate in law creation and application as well in psychological processes concerning the understanding of the integral character of law. This is a more humanist (Lat. *humanus*) or individualist orientation towards comprehending law but then when law is concerned one cannot deal with it without its social dimensions: *Ubi societas, ibi ius*. Both individual and social dimensions concerning law are necessarily connected: there is no individual without society as well as society without its individuals. Without individual people as a society's parts there is no society. Still the present theory tries to understand law as a social phenomenon through the eyes of an individual. Behind a specific group of people which makes or applies law there is always an individualist perspective. Everyone who creates and applies it is at first an individual and only then a member of a society.

The psychological perspective that I am referring here in trying to understand and show in what manner people create and apply law has been taken from Jungian psychological typology and his psychological types. Therefore the necessary social dimension of law has been seen through the eyes of an individual for whom what is typical is the four-type structure. Jung had travelled quite a lot around the world and on the basis of his contacts with local people in different parts of the world he came to a conclusion that the form-type cognitive structure in an individual is universal.

There are, however, differences as to how the relations between specific elements (i.e. the four-type cognitive functions) are arranged within one personality or personalities constituting a particular society. Also law as a special social phenomenon could have its own specific typological structure when it is compared with other social activities, disciplines and sciences. However, such can only be determined to some very broad framework and essentially varies from time to time and from place to another place. But the fact that there might exist a specific general pattern of the psychological types, although quite abstract and general, which is typical of law make the present theory of law particularly interesting.

Concerning an ontological understanding of Jungian cognitive types there is an idea that they are based on a pattern of ontological fourness or quadralism. The four cognitive types would correspond to four ontological principles. The four cognitive functions being of equal value among each other can then be grouped into the dualism of the two poles of the rational (evaluation) versus the irrational (perception). They are however not strictly divided but are in a polar relation. A nice description of methodological polarity where being and the ought are of equal value and in a relationship of reciprocity one may find in Kaufmann (1993: 130).

Although in the structure of ontological quadralism all the four cognitive functions are of equal value, at every moment and in every situation one of these four principle predominates over the other three (i.e. according to Jung there are the superior, the secondary, the tertiary and the inferior functions). To be more precise, the ontological quadralism with all the four cognitive functions presupposes that, first, *in abstracto* they are all of equal value and importance, but, second, in individual and concrete situations subject to time and place, one of them prevails over others. In that aspect it seems that Jung subscribed his theory of psychological types to somewhat dialectics of a prevailing element in their plurality of existence.

How can such ontological quadralism then be understood when applied to the phenomenon of law?

The thinking rational function is undoubtedly the central cognitive function of modern law due to which such as a rule appears in the form of generally written legal norms.[4] Due to this fact even some of the integralists contend that in the context of modern law the normative-dogmatic element prevails despite the co-existence of other elements (i.e. social and ethical). As far as modern law is concerned it is not difficult to agree with them, however, a very important caution must be made: such dimension cannot be isolated from other elements influencing law. In the same manner as rationality that is typical of those cognitive functions that ensure the static element in social relations, such as stability, order, foreseeability, effective resolution of disputes, also legal norms serve the same purpose. In legal norms we can trace the relative autonomy of modern law that is today present as the following elements: abstractness, generality, formalization, hierarchy, systematization being those necessary elements usually typical of a comprehensive system. Without having a specific form (today mostly in writing) law looks to us moderns like lacking certainty so much needed for law in the modern context of fast changing societies.

In dealing with this static, formal, and normative-dogmatic aspect of law that is most typically presented in the legal norm (be it as a legal principle or legal rule), and is primarily a result of the activity of the thinking function, the question is when we actually still discuss the normative legal element in law and not already beginning to deal with legal value or legal interests. A clear line is impossible to be drawn between the mentioned elements in law but for the purpose of this work I could make the following propositions: (a) the normative-dogmatic element is most evidently presented in legal norms; (b) this predominantly applies when we deal with formality of law, and (c) it rather represents the static element in law.

---

[4] The same appears in Visković (1976) while Reale seems to point to value as the ending point (Moreira Lima, 102).

Fig. 4.1 The three-dimensions concerning the static-dynamic (evaluation-perception) dichotomy in law

In the legal norm as a typical expression of rationality, which certainly results from thinking as the predominant cognitive function in modern (at least Western) law, also two auxiliary cognitive functions participate, namely sensation and intuition. These decide whether a legal norm is more interest or value oriented. To an important extent they determine the substance of it so for this reason they could be determined as dynamic components in law.

Below there is a general figure demonstrating the relations of the three components in the framework of the three-dimensional theory of law understood through the prism of psychological typology (Fig. 4.1).

As already mentioned in connection with Jung's psychological typology which has been developed by other scientists, psychologist Quenk indicates several facets that are typical for individual cognitive functions. To repeat, what are typical of thinking are logic, reasonableness and rationality, understanding, explaining, problem solving, finding a common ground, critique and toughness in deciding and decision enforcing. Then, intuition is represented by abstractness, conceptuality, theory, creativeness and originality, while typical of sensation are the facets of concreteness, realistic, practicality, experimental and traditionality (Quenk 10–11). The mentioned facets enable us to make a fairly firm connection of thinking with general legal norms (like constitutions and statutes) and individual legal norms (in, e.g., judgments, contracts, and wills) as the results of lawyers' evaluative function. In general what is characteristic of legal norms in terms of their formal and (limitedly) substantive appearance is their rational and logical structure. On the top of that legal values (such as justice, equality, peace, dignity, legal certainty, etc.), which are usually contained in abstract principle seem to be more related to the cognitive function of intuition, whereas by definition more concrete and practical facts as well as individual interests appear to be more subject to the activation of sensation.

Accordingly, the thinking-sensational or empiric operation of the psychic functions is directed to peoples' facts and interests oriented activities. In this context legal thinking is here motivated by the external (i.e. sensational) world of legal rules and facts or their meaningful connections. Thereby the whole thinking apparatus is invoked to establish meaningful and necessary relations between facts and norms and between norms themselves.

In the frame of this thinking-empirical phase law is not entirely subject to social interests, as in the opposite case it could simply be equated with politics, but also takes care of its relative autonomous principles and rules constituting as a relatively self-referential system. In such a frame the principle of legal certainty seems to be the basic ground when thinking-sensational or thinking-empirical dimensions of law at issue. Such concern for the relative autonomy of law is for example present in the concept of logical compulsion when through interpretation or argumentation we try to justify a logically grounded legal decision and present such, as efficiently as possible, as a (logically) necessary solution. Associated with the rationality supported by the empirical world of facts and valid legal rules are in particular the values of certainty, security, categorical self-sufficiency and formal limitedness

In the process of such empirical-thinking dimension referred to law also intuition has its place. As mentioned above, it can be expressed in this context as extravertive or introvertive intuition. As extraverted intuition it is in the service of a (faster) search for appropriate (empirically expressed) legal norms in order for them to be applied to certain facts. Such extraverted intuition can also be called "instrumental intuition," whose role is to find a quick (*prima facie*) common ground between a legal norm and a factual situation. Such intuition is in the service of instrumental rationality and is particularly useful for quickly resolving easy or clear cases.

This differs from the so-called creative intuition, which is introverted intuition and is used in the event of intuitive evaluation being often ethical evaluation of existing legal norms. In such a case the matter concerns hard or unclear cases where the legal norm is usually unclear or even non-existing. Such intuition operates through the so-named legal sense (*Gerecthsgefuel*) or sense of justice (*Gerechtigskeitgefuel*) as intuitive dimension necessary for filling in gaps in the law or describing or supplementing unclear legal premises. Through such intuition the sense of justice as a basic moral value enters the thinking-rational-sensational activities of a lawyer. In such a manner conflicts may appear in the legal norm as between the empirical-sensational dimension on one hand and the intuitive dimension of law on the other hand, when we question legitimacy of a certain otherwise correct legal form.

Bellow what follows is another figure of the above-mentioned psychological-typological interpretation of the integral (three-dimensional) theory of law.

I have already mentioned the mixing of rational and irrational elements in the phenomenon of law. In the context of postmodern consideration of law we should also have to take into account its irrational part. The matter concerns what Kaufmann called "to count rationally with irrationalism," when he addressed the tasks for legal theory in postmodern times (Kaufmann 1993). At the same time we have to take into consideration the fact that from modernity we inherited the prevailing of rationality in law, which is still applying today so that in any respect we are compelled to recognize a certain prevailing of the normative-dogmatic dimension of law (in the sense of legal norms) over its value and fact/interest oriented perspectives of law.

In relation to Fig. 4.2 it is necessary to emphasize that legal norms are today the prevailing expression or form of legal thinking. However, such legal norms are not

Fig. 4.2 Psychological-typological understanding of the three-dimensional theory of law

LEGAL VALUES = *intuition* (the ought) – perception

↓

LEGAL NORMS = thinking – evaluation

↑

LEGAL FACTS/INTERESTS = *sensation* (being) - perception

purely neutral but filled with the substance of social interests and facts as well as social values. In this sense Kaufmann's theory of legal norm as a kind of correspondence between being and the ought can be understood as integration, where in the legal norm the ought is represented by the norm in its abstract-general dimension while being by the case in its concrete and individuality (Kaufmann 1993). In such aspect the legal norm serves as a means or medium for resolving methodical dilemmas between the normative (ought) and descriptive (being) dimensions of social reality.

If this terminology of Husserlian dialectics is applied to Jungian typology I can point to the fact that the two (rational) evaluative functions (thinking and feeling) are exclusively present in individuals as predominant functions so they can be understood as contradictory. But they are contrary to (irrational) perceptive functions (sensation and intuition) so their relation is complementary. Furthermore, the two perceptive functions are mutually exclusive and thus contradictory. However, the said contradictions are still resolved and reconciled at the level of a personality (but in an order of precedence following the predominant the auxiliary, the tertiary and the inferior function), in a similar manner such that Reale's separate dimensions of law are reconciled in his (uniform) three-dimensional theory or law.

For Reale, law is always value, fact and norm and the relation between them is formed dialectically. "Although it is true that one of the three dimensions may at one point be prevalent . . . one dimension will always be a function of the other two dimensions." (Moreira Lima 137–38). This is close to Jungian typological dialectics only if it could be understood in the sense of, on the one hand, the order of precedence of the cognitive functions as indicated above and, on the other hand, their correlative connections. Certainly beside similarities between the type theory of law and Reale's three dimensional theory of law there are also important differences, which will be indicated below.

In the continuation we will see how the three-dimensional theory of law can be understood in terms of psychological typology more narrowly, with respect to the processes of law creation and law application.

4.2.1 Law Creation and Law Application

The two schemes of separated processes of using certain cognitive functions in the processes of law creation and law application that follow below are perhaps a bit

Fig. 4.3 A psychological-typological understanding of law creation

Perception: **social interests** + pre-existing legal norms *(sensation)*

+

values *(intuition)*

↓

Evaluation *(thinking)* = **(general) LEGAL NORM**

mechanical and one-sided. But they are indispensable for a schematic analysis and to try to understand the psychological typology aspect of the processes of law creation and law application. My intention here is, however, not to argue with the Kelsen's and Merkel's theory pointing to the fact that it is hard to draw a sharp line between the two processes. I would rather point to the value of recognizing prevailing distinctions between the two processes. In such a manner it would be easier to understand the role of the cognitive functions in these processes (Fig. 4.3).

As a typical process of law creation let us take legislative procedure which as a type of legal procedures is subject to rational considerations and in the psychological-typological sense to thinking as a function of evaluation. From such rational evaluation by the deputies statutory general legal norms stem, which are a consequence of many previous discussions and debates, diverse opinions confronted in parliament, as well as of the following of pre-existing rational legal rules that regulate such procedure, and consideration of various bills prepared by professional bodies of ministries.

In the phase of evaluation rational elements are to predominate but the whole procedure is rational-irrational. It is at least, subordinately, irrational due to the influence of perception which is irrational according to Jungian typology. First, there are people's interests that enter the perception phase, in the preparation of a bill and also when such is debated in parliament, and which are subsequently expressed in general legal norms.

Social interests, which seem to be the most important element of the sensation cognitive function in the law creation process, as social facts which are externalized when they are expressed by individuals or groups at the level of society or through their representatives in parliament are initially perceived on the basis of the sensing function (e.g. various opinions communicated are "heard," relevant political materials "seen and read"), and subsequently worked on by thinking when debated by the deputies.

This does not mean that such interests have not been previously (rationally) thought of by their proponents. Certainly they have been. My intention here is, however, only to point to predominance in that procedure of either perception (be it intuition or sensation) or evaluation (feeling or thinking) in a particular phase of proposing a decision and dismissing such. Any social interest could also be based on a certain value accessed to an individual through intuition, but its predominant role is practical and very concrete: to express an opinion however obtained (even thinking is involved) to the society, through the sensing function. As already mentioned the gist or all importance of specific cognitive functions is in their predominant role with respect to other functions.

Let me give one example. Parents with younger children would like that their parenthood would count more than perhaps before, with respect to their tax returns each year so that at the end of the year they would pay less income tax then the previous year. In such a manner they could afford their children not only more material things but also more time since they would need to work less. What is behind that "material" interest is also a purely moral or value of the parents' spending more time for the upbringing of their children. In terms of psychological typology they came to this idea through their intuition by perceiving the moral value of their children's well-being. They intuited, and then also, normally, thought of that their financial "investment" in their children could also be of an interest to the society. So the society should take that into consideration in contrast with those adults without children, and perhaps increase their tax exemptions. We could see that in that process intuition and thinking were also participating, but it is predominantly sensation that made this parents' idea possible through a special interest of such parents that was expressed in order for a potential statutory amendment to take place. In such the greatest emphasis from all the cognitive functions was on expressing the interest being somewhat external expression of someone's will.

Thus, such process of creating laws is irrational-rational and involves various interests of individuals, deputies, narrow social groups and also general social interests. When adopting legal norms in the legislative procedure also higher legal norms need to be taken into account. Also these higher legal norms are in the first place perceived by sensation and subsequently contemplated upon by thinking. It is somewhat different with values which are also reflected in legal norms, general social values, or specific moral or legal values. These are of a more internalized character than interests. What is in this context in play is the irrational intuitive function with subsequent inclusion of the thinking function, which evaluates such intuitive "ideas" and properly places them in the legal norm.

The result of such a typical legislative procedure of law creation are legal norms as a consequence of the rational thinking's analysis and evaluation, which also encompass the elements of irrational sensation and intuition through which interests and values enter the evaluation-thinking process of law creation.

Let me show the above-presented psychological typology of the legislative procedure with respect to another specific case. Suppose that due to a low birth rate in Slovenia there appears a discussion in the society of amending the statute allowing the artificial termination of pregnancy, proceeding in the direction of making the conditions for such far more strict. Suppose there came out of this discussion even a relevant bill prepared by certain political parties, and was submitted to the legislative procedure. Prior to the bill and also during the legislative procedure, two important values would be in conflict: on the conservative side, the value of the fetus' life and on the liberal side the value of the mother's freedom to decide to have an abortion. These values, first intuitively perceived in individuals, will try to be implemented in the legislative procedure through various interests for and against stricter legislation. These interests will be expressed to

Perception: legal facts (of the case) + (general) **legal norms** *(sensation)*

clear cases *(extraverted intuition)*

unclear cases *(introverted intuition)*

↓

Evaluation ***(thinking)*** = **(INDIVIDUAL) LEGAL NORM** (judgment)

Fig. 4.4 The psychological typological understanding of law application

the deputies by proponents or opponents of such a bill through the predominantly sensing function in order to persuade the deputies to vote for or against the proposed solution (in oral conversations, public speeches in parliament, in articles, debates, etc.). In the context of dealing with such amendments also the constitutional provisions and the decisions of the constitutional court or the supreme court should be taken into consideration. Certainly after the perception phase also the thinking and evaluative processes are important due to which the entire law creation process is irrational-rational. However, within the perceptive phase evaluation is somewhat subordinated to perception which gives necessary substance to the process of thinking. After the perception phase what follows is a thinking-evaluation process in the framework of which the amendment to the act on exercising free will of parents on the birth of their children is adopted or refused.

Furthermore, in the continuation let us see how the process of law application can be understood in the light of psychological typology (Fig. 4.4):

In this situation I take as an example judicial proceedings the result of which is the judgment as individual legal act. Also in this case it concerns a rational procedure (of evaluation) in which the thinking function predominates the result of which being the judgment as an individual legal act (containing individual and concrete legal norms). First, such a rational procedure begins with the perceptive phase in which the irrational elements of sensation are present in the sense of perceiving (e.g. hearing, watching, reading) the facts of the case and the relevant legal norm. When a clear case is concerned sensation is then supported by extraverted intuition as instrumental intuition the role of which is to quickly (*prima facie*) guess (or find) the relevant legal norm on the basis of the facts presented. In clear cases, in which both premises are relatively complete and understandable or clear there follows rational evaluation on the basis of making a legal inference. However, when unclear cases are at issue, in which most often the upper premise is not clear and needs to be additional determined by a creative act, there could also be applied introverted intuition, in which by means of a certain legal value or principle intuitively perceived and then thought upon the upper premise is tried to be supplemented and finally determined and then applied in a syllogistic conclusion.

Let this be illustrated by an example. A clear case would be deciding on the criminal offence of theft under the circumstances in which there is clear evidence that the perpetrator stole a coat in a supermarket whereby he even admitted the criminal act. The elements of the sensational perception of this event are facts which the judge learns through the prosecutor's indictment or another kind of charge in which there are relevant facts and evidence as well as relevant legal norms. Such a prosecutorial act leads the judge instrumentally-intuitively, by consulting his prior knowledge of law, to the idea of whether the prosecutor chose the right legal norm of the Penal Code which punishes theft. At the same time the judge normally also perceives the legal norm by his or her senses. Then the thinking-logical process of deliberation or evaluation follows the consequence of which is, e.g., a judgment of conviction given the clearly established facts and the presented evidence. The judgment is a result of a predominantly rational procedure of evaluation in which also the judge's irrational cognitive functions took part.

In the event of an unclear case there could e.g. be a problem with respect to the upper premise in the sense that it would be necessary to establish whether in the case of unjustified use of the internet the matter could also concern an illegally appropriated object or thing and that that could also represent theft. Here the judge could resort to making an analogy, by means of his intuitive function in order to find if he or she can evaluate similar cases similarly. Once he or she establishes the upper premise by aid of analogy there follows the classical evaluative (rational) procedure of deductive syllogism.

Having demonstrated how the process of law application can be read in terms of psychological typology, in the next paragraphs I turn, more narrowly, to how judicial decision-making can be seen from the view of Jung's psychological typology.

4.2.2 *Judicial Decision-Making*

The above-mentioned description of psychological typology is relevant to this inquiry in order to demonstrate that every person is (ir)rational due to his or her basic cognitive functions. This certainly applies to the lawyer and their decision-making, as well as to the judge's deciding. However, the fact that in the lawyer's personality the rational part (i.e. thinking and judging as ideal psychological type preferences) prevails or should prevail certainly importantly contributes to the role that law has had throughout history in society, in which it has ensured at least a certain degree of the rationalization of ever dynamic social relations. From that it follows that the lawyer's cognitive functions are both rational and irrational but the rational elements should predominate. This applies even more to the judge who, in my opinion, is the central figure in the legal profession.

Likewise, the process of discovery, as the initial part of the legal decision-making process according to legal argumentation theory, not only includes rational, i.e. evaluative, elements but also irrational elements since the judge's rationality (i.e. thinking as the predominant cognitive function in legal decision-making) needs certain data or material to begin its evaluation, which receives it through the operation of irrational sensation (i.e. the perception of facts and existing laws) and intuition (i.e. the recognition of the "right" legal norm that is based on certain facts, and the so-called "sense" of justice).[5]

As already indicated, intuition has an important role in legal (or judicial) decision-making. First, it appears in the form of instrumental intuition, by virtue of helping the judge find or recognize the most appropriate legal standard (be it a legal rule or principle) in the legal system to be applied to certain facts of the case. In such an event, this instrumental intuition ("instrumental" hunch) is subject to the so-called internal justification of a decision, as the necessary rational experiment that is necessary for justifying the decision in clear cases. By "internal justification" I understand what MacCormick determined as the first-level or "deductive" justification in which the decision is defended by means of a legal rule and the facts of the case (MacCormick 1978).[6]

Secondly, in the context of their decision-making judges often resort to so-called creative intuition, which is more creative than instrumental intuition as to some extent it exceeds the internal legal system in the event of gaps in the law, ambiguities, vagueness of legal text, implied meanings in it, which are all typical of unclear cases. In such an event, assisted with creative intuition that communicates the necessary information to the judge, he or she must necessarily step from the area of the internal legal system into the realm of the so-called external area of the legal system, whose outer boundaries are the requirements of justice, ethics, morality, legitimacy, (legal) certainty, predictability etc. In this case the decision is justified externally. Here I refer to what MacCormick understood by his second-order justification in which the arguments that are required are to defend the decision by demonstrating that the ruling is in accordance with the prevailing legal order (including in particular legal principles, and arguments from coherence and consistency) (MacCormick 1978).[7]

This entails that such a process often includes intuition – especially if the case at issue is unclear (or hard), which means that the combination consisting of sensation, thinking and instrumental intuition is not sufficient to provide the decision-maker with the necessary material for making a conclusion.

However, the phase of justifying a decision is restricted to the thinking and empirical processes of providing rational reasons for the decision, by way of persuading the legal (and general) audience that the decision-maker has decided reasonably. In such a case, the decision that was reached internally is reviewable externally. Thus, the elements of thinking as rational standards (arguments as reasons; as well as the elements of sensation making the experience of such reasons possible) play an important role as codes that are decisive for the external mediating

[5] I suggest that even in English we cease using the syntax "sense of justice" or "feeling of justice" but begin using the expression "intuition of justice," which is the only right expression according to the understanding of psychological typology by Jung.

[6] *Cf.* Alexy's position that internal justification is concerned with whether the decision follows logically from the premises adduced as justifying it (Alexy 1989).

[7] *Cf.* Alexy's perception of external justification by which he understands the defending of the acceptability of the premises by interpretative methods and arguments (Alexy 1989).

and communicating function of law to be ensured. This phase of decision-making as the phase of reasoning is crucially conditioned by the use of rational codes. This is necessarily so as, unlike reason and rationality, intuition as an irrational cognitive function is incapable of being a mediator, common denominator, or common ground on which people can rely when social disputes are to be resolved.

Accordingly, it seems more than probable that the phases of discovery and justification are to some extent connected, as when one decides in a certain manner they simultaneously intuitively anticipate the justification of their selection of a decision. Nevertheless, it may occur when beginning to write down the reasons for a decision that a judge changes their mind, alter their decision, or selects other reasons than those that they anticipated in the initial reaching of the decision. Therefore, it would be very hard to defend the thesis that the process of discovery and the process of justifying a decision can be rigidly separated. This does not say, however, that certain intuitions, senses, perceptions or hunches concerning a legal decision must not be rationally justified or submitted to a rational "test".

Even though, as Frank alleged, in the process of decision-making the judge's personal (psychological) characteristics play an important role, the decision of the same judge must be reasoned or rationally justified. If this is not possible, they must reach another decision that can be justified (rationally).

If the process of justification is more formal and rational, which is reflected in the use of relatively autonomous legal canons (of positive law or legal texts), to demonstrate that the judge has not acted arbitrarily, the process of discovery is more informal and material. In such, as already above-stated, intuition may play a greater role. As briefly mentioned above, the process of reasoning a judicial decision as the process of justifying such pertains to the type of thinking that is mainly supported by the senses in: (a) perceiving the facts of the case; (b) the norms of the legal text; and (c) expressing the reasons for the decision in the reasoning. Such thinking mainly operates on the basis of codes of positive law, or it tries to be close to that or match that as much as possible. This is the world of more or less formal mechanisms of operative-analytical rationalism and legal logic, which enables a decision to pass the empirical and rationality test, in the context of which the judge tries to remain within the relative autonomy of the legal world. If the decision cannot pass such an empirical rational test, than it cannot be a legal decision.

In addition to thinking, another cognitive function which is more than relevant in the framework of decision-making is certainly intuition. What thus follows is a short presentation of certain (additional) aspects of its relevant role in judicial decision making.

4.2.3 More on the Role of Intuition in Judicial Decision-Making

In order to achieve greater rationality of deciding, the process of deciding itself should be more rationally illuminated. In such a manner it would be easier to understand which psychological factors come into play in deciding. Thus, by also being aware of their irrational part, a judge would adjudicate more reasonably, impartially and objectively. According to Frank, it is in particular the judge who is exposed to emotional dynamism in the court since only an honest judge who is also aware of their competencies, but also of his or her prejudices and deficiencies, can be the best guarantee of justice (Frank 1930: 138). Namely, according to the American Legal Realists, the processes of reaching a decision and justifying it includes the following steps: (a) learning the facts of the case and reflection on a just solution; (b) a hunch or intuition about the solution; (c) examining the possibility of such hunches and intuitions in the framework of an existing law (rules, principles and precedents); (d) reaching a decision; and (e) providing the necessary reasons for the decision (Frank 1930: 138). Thus, as already indicated we can see that both phases (discovery and justification) are mutually related to a significant extent.

A Slovenian legal theorist, Boris Furlan, who lived at the time of the American Legal Realists, has similarly emphasized in his treaties on a theory of legal inferring that, in the process of legal decision-making, a practicing lawyer initially derives from his or her internal (legal) sense. Namely, similarly to Frank Furlan argued that, in contradistinction with the predominantly accepted logical syllogism, a practicing lawyer in his or her logical inferring does not stem from the upper premise of the legal norm but actually from the lower premise of the actual case (state of facts). In this way, he or she uses intuitive recognition in order to find a common denominator between the state of facts and the legal norm which is to be applied. Such an act of intuition leads him or her to the upper premise which is then applied in the form of logical syllogism. However, according to Furlan, the judge must rationally justify or reason their intuition in the framework of logical syllogism, since, as we perceive our world in modern times, *ratio* is the most reliable communicator in our external world, which ensures predictability and necessary frameworks for accepted social norms. If the mentioned recognition is an act of intuition, the syllogism is an act of reason. So that our intuition becomes accessible to other people we must translate it into the form of reasons and rationality. Through logical syllogism alone we cannot find appropriate legal norms that would lead to a solution of the case, but only prove the correctness of that which we found by means of intuition. However, deductive syllogism is the only means of rational proving. Finally, legal syllogism has an undisputed role as providing supervision over our intuitive findings so that they are translated into rational codes (Furlan 2002).

From that we can see that the context of discovery in which, beside (rational) evaluation, (irrational) intuition also plays an important role, cannot be rigidly separated from the context of justification as the latter is often only the necessary result and translation of the former. In the process of deciding itself, when a dilemma occurs because we have addressed a hard or unclear case (with several possible solutions which can all be plausible or when "we ran out of the rules"), we usually pay attention to intuition to provide our thinking with an additional guide for resolving the case. Such intuition could lead to a legal rule, (unwritten) principle, (legal) value, policy, some other standard, helping us to find the legal solution in a thinking "obstacle". However, as above mentioned, such decision that is supported by intuition still has to undergo the (empirical) rationality test, which entails that it is to be rationally and empirically justified in the legal reasoning of the decision.

Undoubtedly the role of (not strictly legal) psychological factors in the work of legislators or those who decide on the application of law (especially judges) is usually proportionate to the openness of legal standards that are the criteria for reaching the decision, as well as to the possibility of broadness of interpretation since such "opened-texture" legal provisions can be reasoned in several ways, all of which can be rationally defensible.

Why does then the thesis of a moderate separation between the context of discovery and the context of justification of legal decisions matter?

Intuition which is mostly used in the discovery context (as perception) is important, even indispensable, for getting proper reasons that are applied in the justification context.[8] After all, legal language is a set of symbols which are to an important extent accessible to us by virtue of intuition. In a legal context this occurs, e.g., when a judge initially, before he or she decides on a case and writes the reasoning, finds an analogy between the text of a relevant legal norm and the language of the facts of the case, or between the material facts of a precedent and the essential facts of a case considered. The CLS and ALR's contribution to a debate in legal theory was important as they demystified the traditional one-sided notion that legal decision-making is entirely rational. Especially the ALR's claim that the judge by the *a posteriori* application of rational arguments often tries to justify the conclusion that was a priori made by virtue of his or her intuition, seems to support the thesis that in reality the context of discovery and the context of justification cannot be rigidly separated. Thus, the irrational part in the discovery context should not be neglected as totally unimportant since this would idealize too much the justification context. Thus, the interest in the discovery context rather than just in the justification context makes the entire adjudication process to appear more real.

However, a mild version of separation between the two contexts is necessary since it is reasons that decide which intuitions are proper for a reasoning, and which are not. For example, in the reasoning of a decision a judge should use so-called social (or objective) reasons, not their personal subjective reasons which could only be a rationalization of their subjective preferences. Finally, the mild separation thesis demands that the discovery context be more rationally illuminated. By being aware of the irrationality (positive and negative) that is present in the discovery context we may reach more reasonable, objective and impartial judicial decisions.

To sum up what has previously been mentioned about the role of intuition in the process of legal decision-making, more precisely in its process of discovery, in the following few paragraphs I repeat what I already said above about the role of the two kinds of intuition in (judicial) decision-making. Moreover, to that I add certain

---

[8] On the importance of intuition in judicial decision-making, see e.g. the book by (judge) Posner, particularly 93–121.

examples of how these two types of intuition are applied in actual cases by legal practitioners.

First, in deciding clear cases so-called "instrumental intuition" seems to play an important role. In such an event, the judge stems from the given facts of a case (i.e. from the lower syllogistic premise) and uses their intuition (so-called "legal intuition") in order to find an appropriate legal norm under which the facts of the case will subsequently be subsumed. If the case is truly clear (e.g. when the facts of the case are well known and the legal norm substantially understandable and determinate, and quite easily found) the judge's intuition is instrumental since it operates as a means, an instrument or "short-cut" to find the relevant legal norm within the relatively explicit legal rules of the (internal) legal system. Such a clear case would, e.g., be when a thief is caught *in flagranti*, when stealing a coat from a supermarket given that his or her criminal intention was clearly established. Within such a decision-making process the judge's initial intuition (also "hunch"), which is irrational *per se*, is rationally evaluated in their mind before it is expressed as a decision, and subsequently also rationally justified in the form of reasons that are provided in the reasoning of the decision.

Second, in the event of an unclear case, the entire process is carried out at the beginning as was mentioned above: (1) the empirical perception (through the judge's senses) of the facts of the case; (2) rational evaluation in the manner of thinking what to do; (3) an intuition (or hunch) as to which legal norm is a possible solution; (3) a rational evaluation as to whether such a legal solution is indeed possible given the facts of the case; (4) the internal decision made; and (5) the decision expressed and reasons for such provided in the reasoning.

If there is no clear upper premise of the legal norm the role of the judge and their intuition must necessarily be more creative. His or her intuition creatively extends beyond the explicit boundary of the legal text into the area of the implicit text[9] of the unclear legal provision, which still must remain within the legal system for otherwise it cannot be a legal decision. An example of such creative intuition is the implicit text of the American Constitution that was discovered in the case of *Griswold v. Connecticut* (381 U.S. 479 (1965), concerning the right to privacy. It is well known that in this case the US Supreme Court found the previously not explicitly existing right to privacy in the US Constitution in the implicit text of the Constitution by virtue of discovering "penumbras" and "emanations" of certain other explicitly mentioned rights (i.e. several amendments to the US Const.). The problem is then how to justify, rationally, such judicial creativity. It seems that the internal criteria of justification cannot be applied so we have to make use of the external criteria of justification, the role of which is to help us establish a necessary connection between the solution and the legal system. Such creative intuition as a form of judges' irrationality is positive as long as it discovers hidden parts, develop undeveloped parts, or upholds or supports parts of the existing legal system. Such creative intuition must still remain within the legal system.

[9] Concerning the meaning of implicit text see Barak 2005: 104–106.

References

Adams, D. M. (Ed.). (1992). *Philosophical problems in the law*. Belmont: Wadsworth.

Alexy, R. (1989). *A theory of legal argumentation*. Oxford: Clarendon.

Alexy, R. (2002). *The argument from injustice*. Oxford: Oxford University Press.

Alexy, R. (2005). Balancing, constitutional review, and representation. *International Journal of Constitutional Law, 3*(4), 572–581.

Alexy, R. (2008). On the concept and the nature of law. *Ratio Juris, 21*(3), 281–299.

Barak, A. (2005). *Purposive interpretation in law*. Princeton/Oxford: Princeton University Press.

Bertea, S. (2009). *The concept of law*. IVR encyclopedia. http://ivr-enc.info/index.php?title=Main_Page. Accessed 5 Nov 2009.

Briggs Myers, I., & Myers, P. B. (1980, 1995). *Gifts differing*. Mountain View: Davis-Black Publishing.

Clark, M. T. (2000). *An Aquinas reader*. New York: Fordham University Press.

Coleman, J. (1996). Authority and reason. In R. P. George (Ed.), *The autonomy of law* (pp. 287–320). Oxford: Oxford University Press.

Dworkin, R. (1986). *Law's empire*. Cambridge: Harvard University Press.

Dworkin, R. (1997). *Taking rights seriously*. Cambridge: Harvard University Press.

Finnis, J. (1981). *Natural law and natural rights*. Oxford: Oxford University Press.

Frank, J. (1930). *Law and the modern mind*. New York: Bretano's Inc.

Furlan, B. (2002). *Problem realnosti prava* [The problem of law's reality]. Ljubljana: Pravna fakulteta in Cankarjeva založba.

Hart, H. L. A. (1994). *The concept of law*. Oxford: Oxford University Press.

Horkheimer, M. (1974). *Eclipse of reason*. London/New York: Continuum International Publishing Company Ltd.

Kaufmann, A. (1993). *Einführung in Rechtsphilosophie und Rechtstheorie der Gegenwart*. Heidelberg: Muller Jur. Verlag.

Kelsen, H. (1945). *General theory of law and state*. New Brunswick: Transaction Publishers.

Kelsen, H. (1960). *Pure theory of law*. Berkeley: University of California Press.

Moreira Lima, A. C. (2008). A Brazilian perspective on Jurisprudence: Miguel Reale's tridimensional theory of law. *Oregon Review of Intl' Law, 10*, 77–138.

MacCormick, N. (1978). *Legal reasoning and legal theory*. Oxford: Clarendon.

MacCormick, N., & Summers, R. (Eds.). (1997). *Interpreting precedents*. Aldershot/London: Ashgate.

Posner, R. A. (2010). *How judges think*. Cambridge: Harvard University Press.

Quenk, N. (2009). *Essentials of Myers-Briggs type indicator assessment*. Hoboken: Wiley.

Radbruch, G. (1946). Gesetzliches Unrecht und übergezetzliches Recht. *Süddeutsche Juristenzeitung:* 105 *et seq*.

Tebbit, M. (2000). *Philosophy of Law: An Introduction*. London: Routledge.

Visković, N. (1976). *Pojam prava: prilog integralnoj teoriji prava* [A concept of law: A contribution to the integral theory of law]. Split: Pravni fakultet.

Zweigert, K., & Kötz, H. (1998). *Introduction to comparative law*. Oxford: Clarendon.

Chapter 5
The Type Theory of Law

Abstract In this chapter I add a fourth dimension to the classical three-dimensional theory of law, namely feeling, and discuss its role in today's law, particularly when it extends to the area of alternative dispute resolution. Furthermore, in the continuation of this chapter I elaborate upon the major elements of what I call the type theory of law and then explain why I consider it to be a general and descriptive theory rather than a normative theory. I conclude the book by presenting the essential elements of a theoretical model of the type theory of law, and then demonstrating how it could be applied in the context of a controversial social, political, and legal issue which arose in an EU country in the area of constitutional law.

Keywords Three-dimensional theory of law • Fourth dimension • Feeling • Alternative dispute resolution • General and descriptive theory of law • Type theory of law in context

5.1 Introducing the Fourth Dimension

When presenting above the interpretation of the three-dimensional theory of law from the perspective of psychological typology, I left out the fourth cognitive function, namely feeling. I somewhat opined at the beginning of my analysis that feeling has nothing to do with law. I thought it was more typical of art and artistic activities. To repeat Quenk, what is typical of feeling are the following facets: (a) empathetic, in the sense that a decision has impact on people and focuses on important values and relationships; (b) compassionate, considering unique and personal needs of individuals; (c) accommodating, in that it values harmony and incorporation of diverse viewpoints; (d) accepting, by using kindness and tolerance; and (e) tender, in the sense that a decision is made on the basis of gentle persuasion and a personal approach so that others' agreement is gained (Quenk 11).

According to Jung, feeling is a rational – and thus evaluative! – function but an antipode to thinking being a logical way of deciding. As an evaluative function it should also serve certain purposes of making decisions. But in what manner, and in what context could it be related to law? To answer these questions we need to juxtapose feeling with thinking with all their facets mentioned earlier in this book

M. Novak, *The Type Theory of Law*, SpringerBriefs in Law,
DOI 10.1007/978-3-319-30643-8_5

and how they are related to the phenomenon of law. Pursuing this task we will realize that by applying the feeling function in our making of decisions we very much follow a process that is nowadays typical of procedures that are alternative to traditional legal procedures, and are more typically designated as ADR procedures (e.g. arbitration, mediation, conciliation). In those procedures, which to some extent have historically predated or have been parallel to typical legal procedures, which I described above when dealing with the phenomenon of harmonic law, the features of feeling presented above definitely influence the manner of the carrying out of ADR activities. Feeling concerns a kind of polyvalent ways of decision-making which is in contrast with the classical way of deciding in law that has mostly been binary (win or lose).

By including the fourth dimension into the three-dimensional theory of law, I am adding feeling to the process of evaluation as an alternative to the binary way of decision-making (typical of thinking) in the process of law application. Be ADR modern or pre-modern, in both situations for ADR to be applied there is a need for previous legal norms (statutory norms or customary legal norms) as the legal basis for this type of legal deciding, in order for ADR to be alternative to them.

Thus this fourth element only affects law application, which will be presented in the continuation. Moreover, if social disputes can be resolved by mediation then we would need no legal norms and legal procedures, consequently neither ADR.

As a matter of fact ADR is global as it is not only typical for Western cultures but even more for the third world, in particular for Far East countries (the cradle of traditional mediation being China, and in view of a relatively a well-established system of settlement in Japan) and Africa. It is not only geographically universal but also historically (its historical origins in China, at Phoenicians and old Greeks), which was discussed in a greater length above.

Below I am presenting a figure which tries to depict the process of law application in the framework of ADR, in which feeling instead of thinking, or at least as an important addition to it, is applied (Fig. 5.1).

To give a short explanation of the above figure, we can notice that in resorting to ADR procedures, in a much simplified way, the perception phase as the starting point that indicates the legal problem could be the same as in the case of standard legal procedures. What essentially defers from traditional legal procedures is the evaluation phase, in which instead of the so-called logical (harder) means

Perception: facts of the case + (general) **legal norms** *(sensation)*

clear cases *(extraverted intuition)*

unclear cases *(introverted intuition)*

↓

Evaluation ***(feeling)*** = **(INDIVIDUAL) LEGAL NORM** (mediation contract)

Fig. 5.1 The psychological typological understanding of law application in the process of mediation

alternative or harmonic (softer) means for dispute resolution are applied leading to a less formal individual legal act such as a (less binding) agreement on mediation.

Moreover, I did not say anything about the role of feeling in law creation processes as one type of the two standard processes concerning law. Here I can say that contrary to a decision to adopt a general legal norm there is the decision not to adopt one since potential or existing social disputes could be resolved to applying other social norms such as moral norms or customary norms.

5.2 A General and Descriptive Theory

Finally, given the above-presented role of the fourth cognitive function and thus application of the all four cognitive functions in understanding the phenomenon of law, I can suggest the following definition of the concept of law: "Law consists of social values and interests that condition the creation of legal norms, which are the basis for formal or informal law application and thus resolution of disputes."

What this definition brings us in the psychological-typological sense of *homo juridicus* are the following dimensions: (1) thinking refers to legal norms and formal decision-making; (2) intuition is related to legal values; (3) sensation represents legal interests and legal facts; and (4) feeling is connected with informal (or alternative) decision-making and also with the option that no legal norms are adopted since disputable social relations can be resolved on the basis of other social norms such as moral and customary norms.

The afore-mentioned is presented below in the following Fig. 5.2:

One could say that the mentioned cognitive functions are not specific for law but participate in every possible situation. That is to say that all these four psychological-type functions apply to other disciplines and sciences as well, not only to law. What is there then so specific for law in order for them to be applied? In

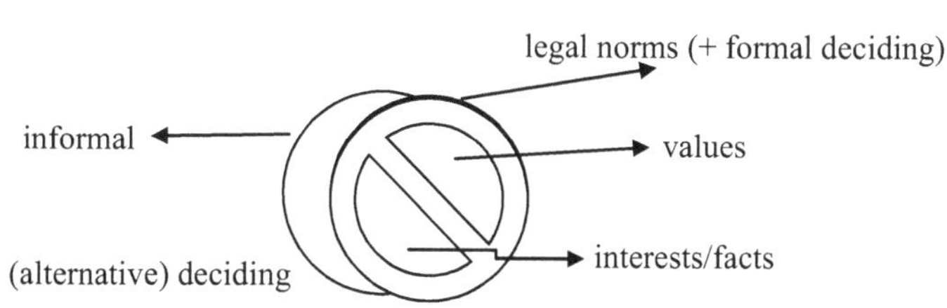

Fig. 5.2 A four-dimensional theory of law

fact the psychological types are universal – in terms of time and place. What is specific concerning them is the proportion, distribution or predominance of each of them with regard to a historical moment and geographical constellation. This also applies to law and its appearance in terms of history and geography. In such a manner we better understand the society, individuals, and law of our time and place, and are able to differentiate them from other periods and places.

What follows below is an attempt to form a unique theory of law based on understanding the phenomenon of law through Jungian psychological types. As already indicated, the methodological approach of relying on Jungian psychological typology is philosophical here. In the continuation we will see that to form a separate theory one needs to make an exhaustive, comprehensive, and sufficiently coherent account of the phenomenon that one is dealing with. This theory of types tends to be universal claiming that such types pertain to all individuals in all the societies in the world, certainly with particular varieties of every respective group of individuals belonging to a certain society. As the types in different societies are present in different combinations, so the laws of such societies differ from one to another. As it was Jung's ambition to develop universal psychological types so a similar ambition is for this theory to create a universal theory of law. Thus the universality of the types has been utilized to try to understand law from a universalist perspective. This certainly discloses those characteristics that different cultures of the world share when law as a distinct social phenomenon is considered. These common characteristics, however, bring with them all the varieties of law that legal history and legal geography (i.e. comparative law) have ever disclosed.

Moreover, where a particular legal system is concerned, this theory of law tends to be general by thereby referring to law in general, addressing general features of law rather than those pertaining to specific legal branches such as criminal law, civil law, constitutional law (e.g. theory of constitutional law). More specifically, within jurisprudence or general legal theory, this theory deals with legal ontology or its standard topic such as the nature of law.

Furthermore, this theory of law based on psychological types is necessarily one among a number of descriptive theories of law. For example, Van Hoecke from the very outset of his methodology of legal research claims that psychological investigations into law, along with sociological, economical, historical and the like studies, are explanatory in nature as they explain the whys and wherefores of legal concepts, rules, principles and constructions (Van Hoecke 9).

In this context it is not its ambition to show how and what law should be, but how the fact that otherwise universal types have appeared in different times and places and have influenced the different nature of law historically and geographically. This theory attempts to present law as it is in different cultures today globally, as well as how it had looked like historically. It is about to develop in the reader a certain understanding about the nature of law, in terms of understanding why is it like it is, and why it appeared as it did in history. In no manner does it intend to evaluate the existing law or the law that existed sometime in the past, although certain evaluations cannot be excluded even from a descriptive theory of law (Dickson 2001). However, in my opinion, for a theory of law to be determined as descriptive such evaluations must be present to a minimal extent when the predominant approach of the theory is descriptive.

To continue with answering the question of whether type theory could be a descriptive or normative theory of law, let me emphasize again why this type theory of law could not be a normative one.

It could perhaps be considered normative in some very general sense – at least in the sense of comparing the type theory of law as an integral or inclusive theory law with an exclusive theory of law. In that sense, a proponent of the type theory of law (in fact the proponent of any inclusive theory of law) would – normatively – argue that, in comparison with an inclusive theory of law, an exclusive one is reductionist. This is because it finds the essence of law in only one dimension or element, for example either in positive law or in natural law, and that for a proper account of law any theory should take into consideration at least two dimensions, usually positivist and moral ones, in order to be epistemologically satisfying.

The same would apply with respect to the type theory of law as presented here. According to it, in order to have a proper account of law we need to take into consideration the fact that human perception is both sensatory and intuitive. In order to upload our evaluative thinking "processor" with all of the possible information for decision-making to follow, and we would certainly like to have as best as possible situation epistemologically, we should resort to our both perceptive functions: sensation and intuition. It was presented above that the sensation-relevant information would stem from positivist law, while the intuition-relevant information would in this case be moral intuition. In such a manner we come to both types of thinking: empiricist and intuitivist thinking, which to some extent are present in every human being. How then would such an inclusivist aspect appear normatively with respect to an exclusive perspective?

A more extreme example, as already mentioned at the outset of this book, comes from Gustav Radbruch and his famous formulas of non-law and unbearableness (Radbruch 1946). As it is well-now he (normatively) claimed that a valid (positive) law, such as, e.g., the Nuremberg Nazi racial laws, should have been declared non-law in a situation in which such unbearableness was contrary to some basic principles of a civilized society and its morality. In accordance with Radbruch, such unbearableness should be quite high which probably would not be the case in a "normal" everyday situation of a modern democratic and rule-of-law state. In the light of the above-presented "typological normativity," Radbruch's formulas would be interpreted as having a person who, on one hand, faces sensory perceived positive law and, at the same time, perceives it intuitively by means of his internal values as being in extreme violation with his conscience. His conscience follows internal moral values with which positive law comes into conflict.

Radbruch's position applying his formulas can be designated as a normative position since in such a situation it is not difficult to admit that internal moral values, intuitively perceived, justify a reaction against such violations of civilized principles by positive law. In an extreme situation of Radbruch's kind, even the type theory of law can be understood as a version of a normative theory of law. In a "normal" democratic situation this is much more tricky and complicated.

Since the example of resorting to Radbruch's formulas is a rather extreme one, we can try the potential normativity of the type theory of law on another more regular example. Here I resort to the argument of a hermeneutical circle to deny the feasibility of the exclusivist theory of law on the basis of realistic – and thus descriptive – foundations of the type theory of law. Unfortunately I am not able to justify this theory of law in a "normal" democratic situation on normative grounds.

Here the views of a hermeneutic or interpretative theory can be illustrative in a situation in which the (sensorially accessible) legal text is very broad and allows for different positions of, e.g., constitutional-court judges that are to an important extent in their interpretation and decision-making based on their value systems which is accessible to them intuitively.

In that sense they cannot stand out of a hermeneutic circle which consists of legal norms, in this sense most often in the form of constitutional provisions, that are at the level of adjudication sensorially perceived by judges. To constitute a hermeneutical circle in the process of a logical syllogism consisting of legal norms and actual facts, the judges add their intuitions on the basis of which they incorporate their value systems into decision-making. This hermeneutical circle is normally wider in the context of constitutional adjudication than it is in regular court adjudication since in the first example the upper premises of the constitutional-court judges are often broader and more ambiguous that in the second case.

Therefore, it would be realistically wrong to completely deny the role of values (and their being perceived by judges' intuition) in judicial decision-making since thereby we would deny the existence of a hermeneutical interpretative circle, which nowadays seems to be more or less accepted, in contrast with the onetime existing school of mechanical jurisprudence. In such a case it would be very naïve, or legally formalistic, to argue that these judges acted entirely neutrally by their (thinking) evaluation having been only based on the sensorially perceived legal text.

But the situation can be reversed when a constitutional-court judge is intuitively forced to have a particular opinion which is not supported by the text, or is even contrary to the text, so he or she is normatively compelled to follow the text. So despite his (intuitive) hunches he had to yield to an evaluation which is more in the direction to his sensory perception of the legal text.

So is the above-mentioned enough to have a normative account of law?

I do not think so. It is normally possible to describe normative situations and normative decisions but a normative theory of law seems to need to develop a theoretical mechanism for giving precedence to either of the two great perspectives on law: positivist or moralist. It is not enough to only suggest that both views might have something relevant to say. Even if admitting the presence of both views (or in our case the typological perceptions) a normative theorist must develop certain principles or rules to demonstrate when, e.g., the sensory perception (or perception of positivist laws) must yield to (moral) intuition. A descriptivist would only observe that it is possible to use moral intuitions as the decisive basis for taking a legal position in hard cases more than in other easier cases. But it is still very difficult to say whether, when, and how one should do that, which is a task for a normativist to do.

Last but not least, stemming from the example of two constitutional-court judges interpreting the principle of equality with a conservative basing his value-approach on proportionality and a liberal on egalitarianism, in the next chapter, I might be able to describe how constitutional-court judges act in fact (or realistically) when they deal with hard questions. Descriptively at least, it is possible to assert that when such a hard case occurs they (tend to) use their intuition. However, based on type theory I am unable to show normatively what kind of intuition they should apply when such a situation occurs: to assert that they should apply proportionalistic values or egalitarian would be contrary to democratic plurality. Further, a normative position would be that such positions should at least be balanced or that there should exist a system of checks and balances as it is impossible to fully rely on judges' self-restraint.

5.3 The Type Theory of Law in Context

As already mentioned, the four-dimensional type theory of law embraces four different dimensions of law that are importantly associated with Jung's four cognitive functions. They have a slightly different impact on legal outcomes depending on whether the matter concerns the process of law creation or the process of applying law. In both situations, however, we will see that the two perceptive functions have a more substantive dimension in law whereas the evaluative functions are more procedural.

Below I present a theoretical model of how the type theory of law sees the importance of the four cognitive functions in the processes of law creation and law application, as the two main processes in law in general. After presenting this theoretical model in the next paragraph, in the continuation I will demonstrate how this model can be applied in the practical context of a particular legal case from the area of constitutional law in order to describe how the psychological typology may determine the outcome of the case, at least to some extent.

What is typical for the (I) process of law creation is the "operation" of the four cognitive functions in the following manner. Here I give an example of legislative procedure as one of the major procedures of creating law. Firstly, the collective 'sensations' of deputies, particularly in the form of (individual or social) 'interests,' as (substantive) perceptions of their will that is appropriately expressed, are translated into general legal norms (statutes). Secondly, these interests are presented in the context of a rational legislative procedure by means of various debates, deliberations, and finally voting which we can associate with the thinking function. Thirdly, what are also relevant in parliamentary (thinking) procedures are the deputies' intuitions on the basis of which they not only bring into the deliberation their materialized (or "external") interests but also their (internal) values which they come into contact with on the basis of their (introvertive) intuition. On the basis of their perception that has been "filled" through their cognitive functions of sensation and intuition, upon proper evaluation in the form of thinking about a possible solution, they perhaps take a "legalistic" (logical) decision by virtue of which the governing coalition of political parties outvotes the opposition parties who otherwise do not support such a decision. It is considered a formalistic and legalistic decision because of its binary character: it gives the possibility of either "in favor" or "against," which is adopted on the basis of parliamentary rules for voting (e.g. a simple majority of votes of those deputies present).

Instead of making a formalistic and legalistic decision the deputies might, fourthly, take a different turn on the basis of utilizing their feeling function, and reach a more comprehensive and socially harmonious decision. In such a manner the majority of deputies would not simply outvote the minority but would try to reach a compromise that is inclusive of the minority's opinion. In such a manner the deputies might supplement the proposal of the majority by an additional or altered legal provision to satisfy the viewpoint of virtually every deputy. Certainly it is utopian to expect that there would be consensus reached on such a basis in the parliament. Yet a more comprehensive or complex approach to the matter at hand would safeguard at least a qualified-majority decision, which would have a better (more legitimate) impact on the society than the decision reached upon by a simple outvoting.

Moreover, in the context of the (thinking) decision-making procedure deputies (should) also perceive pre-existing general legal norms (constitutional and statutory) that regulate the legislative procedure and then "think" by virtue of taking them into account in the evaluation phase of that procedure.

Further, in the (II) process of applying general laws what is typical for the decision-maker, let us say a judge, is, firstly, when using sensation to perceive (a) (legal) 'facts', which in the framework of normative concretization are subsumed under the lower premise of logical syllogism. In a similar manner (b) pre-existing (positive) laws, which have been given by the legislature, are taken through the judge's perception on the basis of his or her sensory function to become part of the upper premise of the logical syllogism.

Secondly, what also enters a law-application procedure in the "perception phase" is the information that the decision-maker receives on the basis of his or her (introvertive) intuition. Here I mainly associate this kind of information with the decision-maker's internal values that in a legal context encompass (legal) values such as legal certainty, justice, equality, human dignity, peace, respect for human rights, or other inner (moral) values (friendship, goodness, help, etc.). When it comes to the area of legal interpretation, it was hermeneutics in particular that has deftly shown how a decision-maker or an interpreter of a certain (legal) text brings his or her pre-existing knowledge with them in the process of interpreting or decision, e.g., in the form of his or her favorite ideas or values. That was also demonstrated quite persuasively by the moral psychologist Haidt in his discussion of the question of why different decent and righteous people take completely opposing decisions (Haidt 2013).

Thirdly, when all the elements of a substantive character are given by means of the decision-maker's perception, in the form of legal facts, legal norms and legal values, what then follows is the mainly thinking-based procedure to apply the general legal acts to the facts of the case, on the basis of which the judge's sensation (facts and general legal norms) and intuition (legal values) are properly evaluated by the thinking function an outcome of which being a judgement (as an individual and concrete legal norm).

Fourthly, as in the above-mentioned case of law creation, here too another possibility of how to evaluate the perceptions received in the procedure of applying law is on the basis of the feeling function. In manner akin to the case of a parliamentary procedure, the result of the evaluation by means of the feeling function is not a formalistic and legalistic judgment in which one party wins and the other party loses, but in the framework of mediation procedure to strike some kind of a compromise between the litigating parties in the form of, e.g., a mediation agreement or settlement.

From amongst many different intellectual influences on my type theory of law I might repeat at least two of them: (i) Jungian psychological typology by applying it to discussing the concept of law; and (ii) Reale's three-dimensional theory of law, which by having attached to Jungian typology for the purpose of forming my own theory of law I actually altered and extended in several directions. Of these, at least four different or additional elements seem to come to the fore: (a) I have added two-stage integrality: perception (substance) and evaluation (procedure); (b) I have pointed to a cascade of typologies meaning that, procedurally, the two-stage model of perception plus evaluation repeats several times in the processes of creating and applying a legal norm; (c) I have partially changed Reale's social element in his definition of law's three-dimensionality, i.e. social interests and social relations, to also include (legal) facts and also pre-existing legal norms; (d) I have understood Reale's normative element more in a procedural manner, which is typical of a legal way of making decisions in the framework of legal procedures, where usually a general legal norm is applied in order to come to a conclusion thus creating an individual and concrete legal norm (in a judgment); and finally (e) I have added a fourth element or dimension to broaden the definition of law also including ADR procedures.

Here I should stress once more that all the elements and categories that I use to typologically describe the processes of law creation and law application are far from being strictly separated. To claim as such would even be absurd if you subscribed to the idea of integrality.

For example, when a judge receives a case to decide upon, he or she first learns of the facts of the case on the basis of his or her sensation function, then he or she thinks what that means in terms of the (general) legal norm, which he or her thean becomes acquainted with on the basis of the sensing function by reading it. Prior to reading that legal norm, the judge usually uses his or her extraverted intuition to get some quite quick information about a proper legal norm and thus the legal consequences of such facts. In order to come to a final decision he or she then also thinks more thoroughly and might also think while mixing his or her thinking function with feelings as to how such a case could be settled.

The idea presented in the preceding paragraph is that all these cognitive functions are in reality mixed together to present the judge as an integral personality or the judicial proceeding as an integral and comprehensive human activity. The same issues regarding the peculiarities of a judicial proceeding could also apply to a legislative procedure or to any other legal procedure, perhaps in a different order of precedence of applying the cognitive functions.

Even though I am aware of the problem of separating the cognitive functions in the context of a legal procedure, I have nevertheless focused on the following distinct categories: perception: sensation (interests/facts; and general legal norms (statutes, constitution) – and we could add here also courts' precedents); intuition (values); evaluation: thinking (making individual/concrete legal norms), feeling (alternative deciding), for reason of showing predominant elements in that how our cognition works when we deal with law, as typical situations pointing to a particular cognitive element that seems to be the most important for a particular phase of our cognition. In such a manner we are better aware of what is really going on in various legal procedures and with individuals dealing with law, and that can also be of a very important practical value.

Now I turn to applying the above-presented theoretical model to discussing a particular constitutional case, a complex legal and political issue that the Slovenian people have faced in recent months and on the acceptability of which they have been called to decide on a referendum. It concerns the possibility of entering into a legally recognized marriage for gay people.

The whole issue began a few months ago when the ruling political coalition of leftist political parties managed to amend the provision of the Marriage and Family Relationships Act which had determined that marriage could only be entered into by a man and a woman, into the possibility that marriage can be entered into by two persons (regardless of their gender). The bill was initiated by a radical-left opposition political party, who managed to win the support of the largest coalition political party, and was eventually enacted following a summary procedure in the National Assembly. The use of the summary procedure was justified by arguing that the matter concerned a minor change in the act as only few words were changed in the statute.

In order to understand the above-mentioned legislative amendment typologically, or in line with the type theory of law, I could reflect on this (I) procedure of law creation (referring here to the legislative amendment to the general legal act (i.e. statute)) in the following manner. In the framework of the (a) function of sensation, with which I have associated social interests asserted in the framework of that parliamentary procedure, I should refer to two opposing and quite well-known (social) interests in this case: firstly in favor of the change to allow gay marriage arguing that gay people as a social minority should not be discriminated against by a social majority, who, secondly argue that these gay marriages are unnatural and detrimental for those children that might be adopted by such people once married. In such a collision of the two social interests presented by the political parties representing different social groups, considering the fact that the strongest ruling political party of more left-wing orientation supported this legislative change, the proposer of the amendment succeeded in securing a majority of votes for adopting such a change.

What was also relevant in this case for the application of the deputies' sensation function was also their perception of the previous legal regulation of this issue in the marriage act, which was as I described above.

Further, when the matter is considered typologically, we can also see how two different sets of values (associated with the deputies' (b) (introvertive) intuitions) have also collided in the parliamentary procedure when the deputies became acquainted with the proposal of an amendment based on the described social interest. The supporters of gay marriage stemmed from the principle or value of equality in the egalitarian sense in order for this kind of minority to be accorded exactly the same rights to marry as the majority. However, the opponents of the legislative change were against it following (or perceiving) the principle or value of proportionality, as one version of the principle of equality, on the basis of which the said minority should be recognized the right to marry to the extent that is proportionate with their number in the overall number of the entire population, which perhaps would allow them social rights, inheritance, and other rights that are otherwise associated with the marriage, but not the right to a full marriage symbolically in terms of having the same ritual.

Moreover, the (c) thinking function is represented by deliberation and decision-making in the context of the legislative procedure which is regulated, in general, by the Constitution and, in more detail, by the Standing Orders of the National Assembly. On the basis of the deputies' perception (via their sensation) of the interests and intuitions behind their different position towards allowing gay people to marry, as well as their sensation (aided in that by their thinking) about the pre-existing relevant statutory and Constitutional norms, in the process of thinking a new statutory norm in the form of allowing gay marriage was reached.

In line with the four-dimensional integral type theory of law, where does (d) feeling fit in the context of such a legislative procedure? Well, in the case at issue feeling could have been relied on in order to reach some kind of compromise in the parliament that would not entail over voting, perhaps postpone the final decision on the matter instead of using the summary procedure by following a regular parliamentary procedure in which there would be more room for an extensive social debate on the problem of gay marriage which subsequently could have reached a greater support in the parliament. Otherwise the opposition was of the opinion that the coalition simply took advantage of a summary procedure to enact that amendment by arguing that the use of that procedure was justified by a small change to that act as only few words were in fact replaced in that statute. For the opposition that was nonsense and simply proof of having taken the advantage of the coalition's greater number of votes.

What followed the adoption of this legislative change in the National Assembly was the fact that more than 40,000 people signed in support of a referendum against this legislative change, which is possible according to the Slovene Constitution. This request for a referendum was, however, subsequently refused in the National Assembly so the proponents of the referendum required that the Constitutional Court decide on the unconstitutionality of this request for a referendum.

So now I turn to the procedure of a constitutional review of this request for the review of the (un)constitutionality of the National Assembly's refusal of the request for a referendum, and in the framework of this to a (II) procedure of applying law, to see how this process appeared typologically according to my type theory of law.

Initially, from the perspective of the function of (a) sensation, what the Constitutional Court judges initially perceived was the proponents' of the referendum request to review the constitutionality of the National Assembly's refusal of their right to a referendum. I have already emphasized that in the context of law application what is relevant in this respect are the facts that follow from the application to a court. However, when the matter concerns constitutional review, what are considered as the lower premise of logical syllogism are statutory norms, as subordinate legal norms in comparison with constitutional norms at the upper syllogistic premise, which are also experienced first by sensation in the decision-making procedure. Thus the Constitutional Court judges had to "sense" what the proponents' request included, namely the whole material in that request including the allegedly violated constitutional norms, statutory norms, reasons for alleged unconstitutionality, and other similar issues.

Then the judges had to begin their process of (b) thinking about the mentioned request by weighing the arguments of the proponents of the referendum against the arguments of the National Assembly that had refused to allow the referendum, and also replied to the proponents' request as requested by the Court, which the judges also "sensed" at first and then "thought about." This kind of thinking and evaluating on the merits of the submitted request was taking place in the frame of a constitutional review procedure, in which it was to be decided whether the National Assembly's refusal to allow the referendum was in conformity with the relevant constitutional provisions. According to such a procedure of constitutional review, a legal decision was to be reached based on the application of legal norms, according to which only one of the parties would be the winner and the other the loser in this case.

However, if the decision could be made on the basis of (c) feeling there would be something of a compromise reached on the basis of which both the proponents and the opponents of gay marriage would also gain and lose something, which would not be a binary (0–1) solution of this situation. Eventually in the context of the constitutional review there is no ADR procedure envisaged, so the judges did not have the possibility to mediate or settle the case. However, the proponents of the referendum could have withdrawn their request to review the constitutionality of the Assembly's refusal of the referendum, and the Court would have discontinued their proceedings, if the opponents of the referendum had perhaps promised to the proponents of the referendum to reopen the legislative procedure and reach a different decision or perhaps follow a standard (three-stage) legislative procedure. Frankly, in such an emotionally sensitive situation for social regulation as gay marriage the possibility of a compromise sounds quite unlikely.

Finally, what is also interesting and perhaps not always disclosed in a transparent manner either in the process of a legal procedure or in the reasoning of a judicial decision is the role of values in the (d) intuition phase of (constitutional) decision-making. We have already seen above from Haidt how important a role values play in our decisions and this is also the case with the issue of the (un)constitutionality of gay marriage. This was actually the most important substantive issue before the Slovenian Constitutional Court in this case too, although it might have been masked by some procedural aspects of deciding about the request of the (un)constitutionality of the referendum. One could have almost predicted how specific judges would decide on this issue based on them being proponents of either conservative or liberal social and political values.

I have already mentioned before that, according to the American moral psychologist Johnathan Haidt, the moral value of equality as fairness can be understood differently by liberals and conservatives. While the first conceives it in a stricter, more literal, or egalitarian way, the second generally understand it as proportionality – according to one's contribution or desert (Haidt, 205–213). When it comes to the issue of gay marriage it is well known that liberals support it whereas this is usually not the case with conservatives. Their different perspective towards this issue can also be understood in terms of their different accounts of the value or principle of equality as fairness, namely the liberals supporting an egalitarian approach more allowing gay people to marry in the same manner as heterosexual people. The conservatives, however, understand the equality principle more in a proportional manner by arguing that members of the social majority must have more rights proportionately to their far greater number in relation to the number of gay people. This does not mean that the rights of gay people should not be equated in a majority of areas of life in society, such as social security, rights from health insurance, inheritance, etc.

In my opinion this actually occurred in the above-mentioned case before the Slovenian Constitutional Court (No. U-II-1/15 of 21 October 2015). In that decision the Court annulled the National Assembly's order refusing the referendum. The Court's decision was voted for by five against four judges. Concerning the importance of personal values in hard constitutional cases, it needs to be taken into account that at least four judges from the majority who voted against prohibiting the referendum had already in a few decisions before proved their more conservative orientation so their vote in this case was no surprise.

The Constitutional Court formally denied that it was really deciding on the constitutionality of this statutory amendment (i.e. to "legalize" gay marriage) since they stressed that they only decided on the unconstitutionality of the prohibition of the referendum. In accordance with Art. 90 of the Slovenian Constitution regulating the legislative referendum: "The National Assembly shall call a referendum on the entry into force of a law that it has adopted if so required by at least forty thousand voters. A referendum may not be called: … on laws eliminating an unconstitutionality in the field of human rights and fundamental freedoms or any other unconstitutionality."

The judges officially argued that they did not allow the prohibition of the referendum to come into effect since the "unconstitutionality in the field of human rights and fundamental freedoms" as determined by Art. 90 has not yet occurred. They would consider it having done so only if they have already established such in their previous decision or if it has already been established by a decision by the European Court of Human Rights.

Although the Court's majority tried to give an impression in the reasoning of their decision that they were deciding in an entirely "value-neutral" manner, their separate opinions to some extent implicitly or even explicitly disclosed the values they pursued behind their formal decision-making, which in my opinion points to the fact that they understood the solution of the problem in the light of the narrow conception of proportionality in equality.

For example, in my opinion the decisive vote in this decision, the judge who previously had in many cases expressed her liberal opinion, this time took a more conservative step. In her separate opinion she wrote among others the following: "I think that it is just and fair that, on the issue whether in the society's legislation there still remains a traditional notion of family, also people at a referendum should express their opinion. Fundamental and deeply-rooted institutions of family law certainly may not be changed in such an "easy" manner as in this case."

Moreover, another judge from the Court's majority in this decision was also quite indicative expressing his narrow vision of equality in this case. He emphasized that in a democratic society it is normal and even crucial that a majority decides upon the rights and obligations of a minority. For that what is crucial is a legislative procedure and inclusion of the public in that especially when the matter concerns sensitive social issues. He continued, such a situation is envisaged by the Slovenian Constitution in which it is provided that a referendum may be called in order for the voters to exercise supervision over the legislature. Thus it is not allowed to exclude the public from a public debate. There is only one restriction determined in the Constitution to call a referendum when the Constitutional Court by a decision has previously established a violation of a human right, against such a decision. But to claim that people are not capable of deciding on all issues that are otherwise regulated by statute, because they can be manipulated, deceived, are conservative, Catholics, and do not want changes, is unacceptable because then they would not be capable of voting either.

The judges from the liberal minority, relying on their broad conception of equality, pointed to that the referendum should have been prohibited since gay people should be accorded the equal right as "straight" people to marry in the fullest extent and to allow a referendum on such a human rights issue entails that this would certainly not be ensured.

To conclude, I do not want to say that the above-mentioned case points to a conclusion that there is no predictability in legal decision-making as to the outcome of such whatsoever and that all legal deciding is arbitrary by definition, but that in particular when the matter concerns hard or unclear cases, i.e. when the legal text is not precise or fully explicit as it is usually the case in clearer cases, personal values of judges that correspond with one or another type of social values could be decisive. This is also one of the reasons why at the highest courts issues are decided upon by panels of judges as a rule since it is expected that they would deal with hard cases, and the rule is that the higher the level of court, the larger the panel in terms of the number of judges. In such a manner, through a confrontation of such judges' opinions basing on the sort of their "checks and balances," intersubjectivity of their interpretation of the legal text is ensured trying to objectify the judges' necessarily subjective readings of the text as much as possible.

Accordingly, among other things this book tried to show that legal cases are dealt with by complex personalities, including all their cognitive functions and attitudes, which have not only negative but also important positive effects for the results of such decision-making. But if we want legal business to be *ars boni et aequi* we first need to illuminate our knowledge of these psychological functions, understand and analyze them, and then know what to do with them for legal certainty and justice to prevail in legal procedures and society in general.

References

Dickson, J. (2001). *Evaluation and legal theory: Or how to succeed in Jurisprudence without moral evaluation (Legal theory today)*. Oxford/Portland: Hart Publishing.

Haidt, J. (2013). *The righteous mind: Why good people are divided by politics and religion*. New York: Vintage Books.

Jung, C. G. (1971). *Psychological types*. London: Routledge.

Quenk, N. (2009). *Essentials of Myers-Briggs type indicator assessment*. Hoboken: Wiley.

Radbruch, G. 1946. Gesetzliches Unrecht und übergezetzliches Recht. *Süddeutsche Juristenzeitung:* 105 *et seq.*

Reale, M. (1977). *Experiencia e cultura*. Sao Paolo: EDUSP.

Reale, M. (2003). *Teoria tridimensional do direito*. Sao Paulo: Editora Saraiva.

Van Hoecke, M. (Ed.). (2011). *Methodologies of legal research: Which kind of method for what kind of discipline?* Oxford/Portland: Hart Publishing.

MIX
Papier aus verantwortungsvollen Quellen
Paper from responsible sources
FSC® C105338

If you have any concerns about our products,
you can contact us on
ProductSafety@springernature.com

In case Publisher is established outside the EU,
the EU authorized representative is:
Springer Nature Customer Service Center GmbH
Europaplatz 3, 69115 Heidelberg, Germany

Printed by Libri Plureos GmbH
in Hamburg, Germany